LIMITING
G O D

LIMITING
G O D

Updated Edition

John E. Hunter

JOHN HUNTER

Foreword by Stephen F. Olford

Fresh Springs Publications
Kingsport, Tennessee

Original cover art by William Bledsoe
Reproductions of this painting can be obtained by writing:
William Bledsoe
P. O. Box 252
Jonesborough, Tennessee 37659

LIMITING GOD

To Jan, who was used of the Lord

to make these books available once again

CONTENTS

FOREWORD

In 1952, J. B. Phillips (famous for his *Letters to Young Churches*) wrote a book called *Your God Is Too Small*, published by The Epworth Press, London. In it the author deals with UNREAL GODS and THE ADEQUATE GOD. I could not help recalling the title of this book as I read again *Limiting God*. While the former work is mainly a message to the unbeliever, it illustrates dramatically how we, as Christians, tend to put God "in a box" by our unbelief.

The children of Israel did this again and again (see Psalm 78), and so did the Jews when Christ was here on earth. We read that the Lord Jesus "could do no mighty work [in Nazareth] . . . because of their unbelief" (Mark 6:5-6). Twice in the gospel records we find Jesus "marveling": He marveled at the "great faith" of a Roman centurion (Luke 7:9); and again, He marveled at the unbelief of "His own country," among "His own relatives," and in "His own house" (Mark 6:4). In this climate of unbelief, the Master chose not to exercise His miraculous power. This is still true today. As Christians, we "limit the Holy One." This is why the church (with few exceptions) is so powerless, and the world is so godless!

It is to this desperate situation that my friend, Dr. John Hunter, addresses his book, *Limiting God*. Every issue he deals with is an aspect of unbelief in Christian life and practice.

I thank God that, through the vision and action of Fresh Springs Publications, reprints of Dr. Hunter's books are being made available to those who "hunger and thirst after righteousness." Having ministered the Word with dear John on a number of occasions, I can "hear" him as I read these chapters. His age and indisposition may prevent him from expounding the Scriptures publicly, but thanks to the republication of his books, we can once again capture his Spirit-anointed ministry in printed form.

I warmly commend this title (and others to come) to Christians everywhere. May we all listen to God saying to us afresh: "Today, if you will hear His voice, do not harden your hearts" (Hebrews 4:7). Do not "limit the Holy One."

Stephen F. Olford
Founder and Senior Lecturer,
Stephen Olford Center for
Biblical Preaching
Memphis, Tennessee

1

Limiting God For Us

The Old Testament is the rich and blessed treasure-house of God. There is comfort and challenge, light and guidance, teaching and direction in all its pages. It speaks much of things to come, it makes many prophecies and promises, but it finishes with a feeling that "this is not the end!"

The New Testament is the glorious complement to the Old. All the promises and prophecies are either fulfilled in it or given a new meaning. The New Testament simply had to be written to vindicate the faithfulness of a Holy God.

But the New Testament by itself is definitely incomplete. Many times we read, ". . . that the Scriptures might be fulfilled"—words that point back to the promises of God. Characters are referred to and incidents recalled in such a way that without the knowledge of the Old Testament, the New Testament could not make complete sense. Each of the Testaments is wonderfully interwoven with the other. There is a family likeness between them. Types are fulfilled, and the most impossible prophecies come true. Through all the writings shines the holy character of the Divine Author.

In 1 Corinthians 10:1-12, Paul refers to the Old Testament record of God's dealings with the children of Israel on their journey from Egypt to Canaan. As he points to their failings and sins, he links us with them in verses 7-10: "And do not become idolaters as were some of them. . . . Nor let us commit sexual immorality, as some of them did . . . nor let us tempt Christ, as some of them also tempted. . . . nor complain, as some of them complained. . . ."

Most certainly the Holy Spirit is challenging us. To make it more emphatic, He adds in verse 11—"Now all these things happened to them as examples, and they were written for our admonition. . . ." In other words, the Spirit points us back to the Old Testament, especially to the experiences of the children of Israel, saying, "All the things that happened to them are examples, or types, of the way you may behave, and they are written for your admonition, or your warning." As we read their story, we will see ourselves today. So let us take warning, lest we too experience the consequences of their failure. If we feel ourselves to be above such weakness, verse 12 tells us, "Therefore let him who thinks he stands take heed lest he fall."

How important this warning must be in the eyes of the Spirit of God. He sends it, not to those who are falling in the Christian pathway, but to those who feel they are continuing to stand. In this way, God uses the records of the Old Testament as a textbook for *personal* Christian living. He directs His warning to "him who thinks he stands. . . ."

Never was there a day when such a message was more needed. The personal life of the believer—the overwhelming need for personal purity and victory—is the greatest priority in the Church today. There never was so much evangelistic activity as there is at the present. The church of God seems alive to this need. In so many ways the message of the Gospel is being sent out. In our own land, every means is being used and exploited. It is comparatively easy to hear the Gospel. But, more and more, I am realizing that evangelism is not enough. I have traveled much, and seen, heard, and noticed—and now I am more convinced than ever that behind the message of the Gospel there must be a walk, a life, of personal holiness and purity. The Lord Jesus said that "by their fruits you will know them" (Matthew 7:20). We often get taken in by the size of the tree, or the wonderful shapes and colors of the leaves, or the glorious display of floral beauty. The Lord said, "by their *fruits*. . . ."

I am more convinced than ever that behind the message of the Gospel there must be a walk, a life, of personal holiness and purity.

It is interesting to examine these verses in 1 Corinthians 10 for Paul's use of pronouns. Sometimes he includes himself as being capable of the specific failure. At other times he points to his readers only as being in danger. In verse 6 he says, "Now these things became our examples, to the intent that we should not lust after evil things. . . ." Here Paul includes himself, recognizing his own potential weakness in this area of temptation. In verse 7 he says, "And do not become idolaters. . . ." Here he excludes himself. The man who could say, "For to me, to live is Christ" (Philippians 1:21), could never be guilty of being an idolater.

In the next verse Paul is again very conscious of his own weak flesh: "Nor let us commit sexual immorality . . . ." And in verse 9—"nor let us tempt Christ"—Paul included himself as a possible victim of this sin. In verse 10 he says, "Neither murmur ye," excluding himself. The man who could say, "I have learned in whatever state I am, to be content" (Philippians 4:11), would never be guilty of grumbling if things went wrong.

Paul sums it all up by saying that all these things are written for our admonition, showing his sense of his own need of the warning. See how this adds much more punch to verse 12: "Therefore let him who thinks he stands take heed lest he fall." Paul had not arrived; he wasn't too big for such a warning. But some of us may be so. We may think our advanced civilization has given us, personally, the answer to moral failure. Not so. It is this kind of thinking Paul warns us about. This is the great message for the church today.

So it is that this message from 1 Corinthians 10:1-12 comes to us with a sense of urgency. Are we, in our day and generation, following the example of the children of Israel? The word is so plain which tells us that these things happened as types. They were written for our warning.

The purpose of this book is to take heed of the warning given by God. We will do as we are told, and look at the recorded incidents to see if there is a message for us.

In Psalm 78, God uses the same method to teach His people of that generation. He shows them the whole story of the children of Israel from Egypt up to their own time. In verses 4-8 we read: "We will not hide them from their children . . . that the generation to come might know them . . . that they may set their hope in God, and not forget the works of God, but keep His commandments; and may not be like their fathers, a stubborn and rebellious generation, a generation that did not set its heart aright, and whose spirit was not faithful to God."

The warnings continue right through the seventy-two verses in this Psalm. Verse 41 seems to gather together the whole idea and to sum up the effect of Israel's failure: "Yes, again and again they tempted God, and limited the Holy One of Israel."

What an unusual thought this is—that these people *limited* God. The Almighty Creator God was limited by the creature. They, of their own free will, shut themselves up in a wilderness. They pushed God into a corner. It wasn't that God was not strong enough or powerful enough, but that His people deliberately chose to limit Him!

They limited God in two distinct ways. First they limited what God could do *for* them, and then they limited what God could do *through* them. In Deuteronomy 1:2 we read: "It is eleven days' journey from Horeb by way of Mount Seir to Kadesh Barnea." But the next verse says, "Now it came to pass in the fortieth year." How amazing! Forty years later they still had not reached the land of Canaan! What could have been accomplished in days was finally completed in over forty years. So the Bible says that they limited God in their progress.

What could and should have been a continuous forward movement—pressing on, counting on God's promise, expecting nothing but blessing—became a dismal failure. Their speed slowed down, and eventually they stopped. They ceased progressing and started to wander. They lost their vision of the Promised Land and were content with a much lower standard. Dissatisfaction, disappointment, disaster, and disobedience became the accepted norm of their daily lives. God was limited.

Out Of Bondage, Into Freedom

Further on, in Deuteronomy 6:20-25, we are told what an Israelite was to say to his son if he asked questions: "then you shall say to your son: 'We were slaves of Pharaoh in Egypt, . . . Then He [the Lord] brought us out from there, that He might bring us in.'"

God's purpose was to deliver His people out of Egypt, and to bring them into Canaan. There was to be a continuous movement, as it were, from Egypt right into Canaan. God's intention was to take them from the bondage and suffering of Egypt right into the freedom and riches of Canaan. *His redemption was not out of Egypt into the wilderness, but out of Egypt into Canaan.*

But again, the Bible says that they limited God—not only in their progress, but also in their possessions. There was so much more that God could have done for them, and was willing to do for them. But they, of their own free will, limited Him. Through their own stupidity, ignorance, and disobedience, they insisted on taking their own way. They disregarded all the warnings of a God who loved them and cared for them, Whose one desire was to bless them—and so they limited Him.

They possessed nothing, although everything was theirs. All the pastures were theirs, pastures filled with milk and honey. All the hills were theirs, hills which gave the metals they needed. All the cities were theirs, cities which contained the houses and furniture they needed. Everything was theirs the moment they stepped out of Egypt. All they had to do was to possess their possessions.

As God said to Balaam in Numbers 22:12: "you shall not curse the people, for they are blessed." They were blessed indeed, but *they wouldn't claim their blessing.* They accepted defeat as the normal way of life. Because of all this, they limited what God could do for them. They made no progress and had no possessions. And the tragedy was that they *chose* to be this way. God could have done so much more, so very much more, but they limited Him and suffered the consequences.

Just as the Word of God summed up their behavior by saying, " They limited God," so it might also sum up Christians' behavior today.

The Word of God in 1 Corinthians 10:11 has been saying to us that we are to look for types of our own behavior and take warning. We can realize now with shock that what the Israelites did is terribly true of many of us. Just as the Word of God summed up their behavior by saying, "They limited God," so it might also sum up Christians' behavior today. Everything we have considered so far can be a type of our own behavior. We, too, have been redeemed from Egypt, from a world which held us in bondage to sin. We have been redeemed by the blood of a lamb—Christ, our Passover, was sacrificed for us (1 Corinthians 5:7). As Deuteronomy 6:23 says, God brought us out that He might bring us in. God's plan for us is a deliverance from bondage to sin to a completely new life in Christ Jesus.

Walking As We Have Received

We read in 2 Corinthians 5:17, "Therefore, if anyone is in Christ, he is a new creation; old things have passed away; behold, all things have become new." If I am a true child of God, then I am *in* Christ. In John 17:20-21, our Lord prayed for us: "I do not pray for these alone, but also for those who will believe in Me through their word; that they all may be one, as You, Father, are in Me, and I in You; that they also may be one in Us . . . ."

If I am a believer on Jesus Christ, then I am in Him. And if I am in Him, I am a new creature, a new creation. Old things have passed away, and all things have become new. Notice, this is true of me *now* according to God's promise: "if anyone *is* in Christ, *he is* a new creation"—not "he will be," but he *is* right now. God brought me out of sin that He might bring me into Christ. He brought you out that He might bring you in.

But so many of us are stuck in the wilderness. All things are ours in Christ but, like the Israelites, we limit God. Just as they limited God in making no progress, many of us are content to have a wilderness type of Christianity. The characteristic word in the wilderness is *wandering*. The children of Israel wandered, sometimes going around in circles. How true this is of some of us, both as individuals and as churches. There can be plenty of activity, much of which at first sight seems good and healthy. But when it is examined for progress in spiritual grace and truth, there is nothing to report. Plenty of leaves, quite a lot of pretty flowers, but no fruit. Why is this so? Simply because we do not go on and make progress.

God's salvation isn't a place or a passage. It is a Person.

There is one verse in the Bible which has meant more to me in this respect than any other. It is Colossians 2:6: "As you therefore have received Christ Jesus the Lord, so walk in Him." It fits in so well with our present thought of progressing into Christ. As you have received . . . so walk. Walking isn't wandering; walking is making progress. Here is the secret of progress: *as you have received, so walk.*

When I came as a sinner to Jesus, I received Him as my own personal Savior. I didn't believe a creed, or join a church, or sign a form. I accepted a Person. "For God so loved the world that He gave His only begotten Son, that whoever believes in Him should not perish but have everlasting life" (John 3:16).

God gave a gift—His Son—and I accepted that gift. I received Jesus Christ. Not only did I believe in His work, but I accepted His Person. God's salvation isn't a place or a passage. It is a Person. So Colossians 2:6 tells us, "As you have received . . . so walk." How did

I receive Christ? I received Him by faith and with empty hands. I did nothing toward my salvation—"not by works of righteousness which we have done" (Titus 3:5). I simply realized my need, believed God's answer to my need, and accepted Christ as my Savior. The moment I accepted Him I was saved, delivered out of Egypt's bondage by the shed blood of Christ. Also, I was in Christ, and because I was in Christ, I became a new creation.

Now that is perfectly true positionally and potentially, but very often it is not true practically. What I failed to do was go on—to walk as I had received. I thought that because I had received Jesus as my Savior, that was that. My sins were forgiven. I was saved, so now I had to be a good boy and live the Christian life. But that is where I got stuck in the wilderness, wandering and limiting God. I thought it was up to me now to live a good life, to do my best to serve Him—but nothing ever seemed to happen. I spent many years wandering in the desert. I wasn't in Egypt any more. I had been delivered, but I found it rather miserable, and sometimes monotonous, living in the wilderness. Sometimes I came upon a little oasis which was very thrilling, but it only served to make me long for more such places.

Then one day God opened this verse to me. As I had received Christ Jesus, in just the same way I had to walk, day by day, *in Him*. I had to *walk in Him, not in the wilderness*. Jesus Christ is Canaan. God brought me out so that He could bring me in—*in Christ*. Praise God, I had discovered the secret of progress! In His mercy, God let me see the simplicity of the whole thing. I just have to walk receiving. When I first came, I received Christ. Now as I walk day-by-day, I continue to receive Him. He is all I need. He is made unto me all I can ever want.

So now my daily Christian life is a moment-by-moment experience of receiving Christ. Whatever problem, fear, anxiety, temptation, or frustration comes into my life, it isn't my job to meet it. My job is to expose the whole situation to Christ Jesus the Lord, and then to walk believing that what He has promised, He will also perform.

This is what God means when He says in 2 Corinthians 5:17 that "old things have passed away; behold, all things have become new." So many of us are positionally and potentially new creatures in Christ, but practically we are still doing the same old things, still wandering in the wilderness and getting nowhere. But all things can become new if only we walk day-by-day, moment-by-moment, receiving "all that He is for all that I need."

The greatest need in the church of God today is that those who profess and call themselves Christians should have a life which backs up the message.

Earlier in this chapter we spoke of the need, not for increased evangelism, but for the life behind the message. The greatest need in the church of God today is that those who profess and call themselves Christians should have a life which backs up the message. "As he which hath called you is holy, so be ye holy in all manner of conversation" (1 Peter 1:15, KJV). When we remember that the word "conversation" means "conduct and manner of living," we find ourselves back to Colossians 2:6: "As you therefore have received Christ Jesus the Lord, so walk in Him."

It is essential that my life should be pure and holy—essential, not optional. If I allow sin, failure, defeat, or any other of the "old things" to dominate in my daily walk, then I am limiting God from beginning to end. If I go on doing this is in spite of His warning, I will make a farce of my Christian walk, a fool of myself, and a friend of the devil.

We have been thinking in this chapter of the tragedy of limiting God in what He can do for us. We have considered Deuteronomy 6:23 where it is recorded that God "brought us out . . . that He might bring us in." Verse 24 goes on to say: "And the LORD commanded us to observe all these statutes . . . for our good always." The whole plan and purpose of God is "for our good always." God never limits His blessings to us. The measure of God's unlimited desire to give is recorded for us in Malachi 3:10: "'Bring all the tithes into the storehouse . . . try Me now in this' says the LORD of hosts, 'If I will not open for you the windows of heaven and pour out for you such blessing that there will not be room enough to receive it.'"

How God longs to give! Listen to God's longings for us recorded in Deuteronomy 5:29: "Oh, that they had such a heart in them that they would fear Me and always keep all My commandments, that it might be well with them and with their children forever!" The tragedy of missing the blessing, of limiting God's goodness, is that it comes through our own disobedience.

2

Limiting God Through Us

In the last chapter we considered Psalm 78:41, where the Lord sums up the ways of the children of Israel in these words: "they . . . limited the Holy One of Israel" (KJV). We thought of this as a twofold limitation: they limited what God could do *for* them, and they also limited what God could do *through* them. Our main concern then was with the idea of limiting what God can do for us. In this chapter, we want to think of how we limit what God can do through us.

We need, first of all, to get our priorities right. If God is limited in what He can do *for* you, then most certainly He will be limited in what He can do *through* you. It was this way with the children of Israel. God could have done so much more, humanly speaking, if He had had the full cooperation of His people. Not only would they have been blessed as a people, but they themselves could have been a bigger blessing to all around. We find that, even when they entered Canaan, instead of being a glorious pure witness to Jehovah, they became followers of the gods of the dwellers in the land.

In our lives this can be true, too. If we are reflecting the joyous blessing of the presence of Christ, then through us God can bring blessing to others. His work will be unhindered because of our positive enjoyment of Christ. If, on the other hand, we are living in our own private wilderness, thoroughly miserable and utterly discontented, no one is going to be impressed

---

If we are living in our own private wilderness, thoroughly miserable and utterly discontented, no one is going to be impressed by the goodness of God.

---

by the goodness of God. To them He will appear very undesirable, all because of our wilderness behavior. We will have limited God's working through us because we have limited what God can do for us.

The Danger of Turning Back

Psalm 78:9 records the way in which God was limited: "The children of Ephraim, being armed, and carrying bows, turned back in the day of battle." Verse 41 says, "Yea, they turned back . . ." (KJV). Verse 57 says again, "But (they) turned back." Three times it is recorded that they turned back. Notice who turned back—it was the children of Ephraim. Ephraim means "twice fruitful"—in other words, those who had a great record of previous service.

Following our instructions from 1 Corinthians 10:11, if we look for examples to instruct us today, the word becomes doubly serious. Here are those who have proved themselves in God's service, those, in one sense, on whom God relies. Could this be any of us who seek to serve, whether in a large way or a small way?

See also *when* they turned back—right in the day of battle. There had been all the talking, all the planning, all the preparation. Then the great day arrived, and just at the critical moment they turned back. No wonder God was limited in what He could do through them. No wonder the words come three times, "Yea, they turned back." It wasn't because they were weak or ill prepared; verse 9 says they were armed and carrying bows. They were fully equipped for offense and defense. In spite of this, they turned back. *They had all the promises of God, guaranteeing them His presence and His power, but they still turned back.* So they limited God in what He could do through them.

Psalm 78:57 says: "But (they) turned back and acted unfaithfully like their fathers; they were turned aside like a deceitful bow." The words "deceitful bow" really mean a "slack bow." The children of Israel were just like a bow for shooting arrows. All the pieces were there—the wooden upright which gave them the tension, the string that thrust forth the arrow—but the whole thing was slack. The string hung limp and useless, and the bow was utterly ineffective.

A slack bow has, first of all, *no power.* The normal bow in actual use releases the arrow with a "ping," but a slack bow has no power. The arrow just goes "plop!" and falls to the ground. Secondly, a slack bow has *no purpose.* The normal bow sends the arrow on a true course, but a slack bow has no ability to keep its purpose. The arrow flies on a wrong course, and the whole action is a failure. Thirdly, a slack bow gives *no pleasure.* Who would want to use a bow which had no power and no purpose? The whole thing is unsatisfactory, and the archer soon puts the slack bow to one side, finding no pleasure in such an object.

The Bible says to us that some of us are like slack bows. We could be so effective in the hands of God if we were not so weak and useless. Slackness in prayer and Bible reading always results in a slack bow—and a slack bow limits God. Remember, too, that "backsliding" comes from "slack-abiding."

But we were thinking of those who were armed yet turned back in the day of battle. How does this apply to us? Are we armed in the day of battle? 1 John 4:4 contains a precious promise: "Greater is He that is in you, than he that is in the world" (KJV). Here is something clear, precise, and definite. Notice first the Person—"greater is He that is in you. . . ." My defense is not my skill nor my studies, but my Savior—a Person. 1 John 5:11-12 tells us quite definitely, "And this is the testimony: that God has given us eternal life, and this life is in His Son. He who has the Son has life; and he who does not have the Son of God does not have life."

My defense is not my skill nor my studies, but my Savior—a Person.

God's Word teaches us that we are indwelt by the Holy Spirit, the Spirit of Jesus Christ. Romans 8:9 is so sure, "Now if anyone does not have the Spirit of Christ, he is not His." If I declare that Jesus does not live in me, then I cut myself off from all God's blessings, for I am not His. Ephesians 2:12 assures me, then, that I am without God, without Christ, and without hope. But, if I recognize the glorious truth that Jesus Christ dwells in me, in the power and person of His Holy Spirit, then my whole world is changed. Then I can say, "the One who is in me is greater."

Recognizing The Enemy

Notice secondly the power. *"Greater is He that is in you than he that is in the world."* Ephesians 6:11-12 calls us to arm ourselves because, "we do not wrestle against flesh and blood, but against principalities, against powers, against the rulers of the darkness of this age, against spiritual hosts of wickedness in the heavenly places."

Your real enemy is not yourself, your boss, your competitor, or your neighbor! Your real enemy is the prince of this world, the devil. Three times our Lord gave him that title—in John 12:31, 14:30, and 16:11. In Ephesians 2:2 he is called "the prince of the power of the air, the spirit who now works in the sons of disobedience." He is the power behind all that is evil— ". . . the whole world lieth in the evil one" (1 John 5:19, ASV). But we rejoice that the One who indwells us is greater than all the power of the enemy. He said, "All power is given unto me in heaven and earth . . . and, lo, I am with you always" (Matthew 28:18-20, KJV).

Notice, thirdly, the present tense. "Greater *is* He." I have Who I need, what I need—*when* I need. Right now, in the arena of the everyday, in the common things of life, I am armed. 1 John 4:17 tells us that "as He is, so are we in this world." "As He is," —not as he was or will be. I can stand now, armed in all the mighty power of Jesus Christ, with all His capacity for victory, with all His capability to overcome. All this is mine *now*.

How much more armed we are today than the children of Ephraim were in their day. Well may we agree with Paul: "But thanks be to God, who gives us the victory through our Lord Jesus Christ" (1 Corinthians 15:57). And yet, we limit God. We, too, turn back in the day of battle, although we are so perfectly armed. Why did they turn back? It wasn't lack of power, for God was on their side. It was just *fear*. Time and again we read that "they were afraid." God could have done so much more, humanly speaking, if His people hadn't been so fearful. His power could have been demonstrated, His glory uplifted, His will displayed. But they limited God through fear.

Here we see probably the greatest cause of our failure. We, too, are afraid. We repeat the text, *"greater is He that is in you, than he that is in the world,"* and then we go and repeat the failure.

The greatest weakness of the Christian church at the present time is the quality of our living. There are too many horizontal Christians.

Here and there, however, in all ages and in all places, God has had His faithful few. There are men and women who have dared to believe that God meant what He said. They stand out like jewels amidst the dust of defeat. It wasn't education that gave them their victory, or ability that took them to triumph, but an absolute faith in an all-powerful God who will always vindicate His promises.

In the world of boxing, a defeated man is often called a horizontal boxer because of his ultimate position—flat on his back. The greatest weakness of the Christian church at the present time is the quality of our living. There are too many horizontal Christians. The word of God repeatedly calls for us to stand. Our faith should be vertical, not horizontal. But so many Christians spend their lives picking themselves up off the floor. They get up to struggle a little more, and then down they go in defeat once again. Sad as it may seem, this is the only life some Christians ever know. And so they come to accept a succession of failures and defeats as the "normal" way of living. How can such a Christian serve God? How can he ever become a conqueror when he is always a casualty? No wonder God is limited.

Cleansed, Then Clothed

The answer to this shameful situation is a better understanding of God's salvation. If we turn to Romans 5:8 we read, "But God demonstrates His own love toward us, in that while we were still sinners, Christ died for us." Notice the past tense in these words. The whole question of my sin has been dealt with. My sins are gone, as we read in Hebrews 10:17: "their sins and iniquities will I remember no more" (KJV). Hebrews 10:14 says, "For by one offering He has perfected forever those who are being sanctified."

For many of God's people, however, this is all they know of God's salvation—that their sins are forgiven. They are like the little children in 1 John 2:12, "your sins are forgiven you for His name's sake." But notice that God never washes us from our sins to leave us in our nakedness. God's word says that we are justified (Romans 5:9). *To be justified means not only that my sins are washed away, but that I am clothed in the righteousness of Christ.* Sometimes a preacher will say that to be justified means to be made "just-as-if-I'd never sinned." Such an explanation is very clever, but it is not really correct. Justification means that I am cleansed, then clothed.

In these days of much evangelism, there is some preaching which falls short of the true Word of God. A message which is only "Come to Jesus and have your sins forgiven" is insufficient in content and incomplete in outlook. Such a message may be used to get quick results and bigger figures, but it will surely produce quicker retreats and bigger failures. Inquirers who are assured that by believing in Jesus their sins are forgiven, and are then sent on their way to live for Jesus, are surely heading for defeat. There is more in God's salvation than having my sins forgiven—much more.

The words that follow Romans 5:8 with its past tense, are "Much more then, having now been justified by His blood, we shall be saved from wrath through Him" (vs. 9). Here is the future tense of my salvation—"we shall be saved." Saved from wrath—there will be no Great White Throne judgment for me. I have a past tense to my salvation and a future tense. This aspect of salvation is called being reconciled to God, to have peace with God through our Lord Jesus Christ. (Notice that we are reconciled to God—God is never reconciled to us. *We* are the guilty party, and we need to be reconciled.)

It would be fairly safe to say that this is what many Christians take as the scope of their salvation. Their sins are forgiven, they have a home in heaven—praise God, how wonderful it is! But just at this point, there creeps in the one thing that limits God. The believer, rejoicing in the knowledge of sins forgiven and a home in heaven, now sets out to do the greatest job of his life—to live for Jesus.

There is more to my salvation than knowing my sins are forgiven and having a home in heaven.

I was like that. I was so grateful to my Savior for my wonderful salvation that I set out to prove my love by living for Him. I rolled up my sleeves and began the greatest battle of my life. I was going to do great things for Him. I was going to fight, to press on, to suffer, to struggle—all for His sake. As I met defeat and disaster, I turned over new leaves and started again in the battle for Jesus.

Saved By His Life

Many of God's dear people today are engaged in that fight. If they suffer, then they are glad to pay a price for Him. It sounds so heroic—to fight for Jesus, to win for Him. But it is so frustrating. The whole tragedy is that *we are limiting God*. There is more to my salvation than knowing my sins are forgiven and having a home in heaven. There is much more than being reconciled to God. God's word says so! "For if when we were enemies we were reconciled to God through the death of His Son, much more, having been reconciled, we shall be saved by His life" (Romans 5:10).

How unusual that sounds! If I asked you how you were saved, you would most probably reply, "I was saved by the death of Christ." Yet in this verse we read that *"we shall be saved by His life."* Is this a contradiction? The answer is that the phrase in the King James version, "we shall be saved by His life," fails to give the real meaning of the original Greek. It fails both in the verb and in the tense. A more helpful translation is that given in the Amplified Bible, which transforms the whole meaning. "We shall be saved (daily delivered from sin's dominion) through His [resurrection] life." The whole idea now radiates power. I see the answer to my struggles, to my fears, to my defeats. God's salvation has a present tense. Not only does it have a past tense of sins dealt with, and a future tense of a home in heaven, but—what I need most of all—a present tense in my daily living.

Several years ago I was counseling Jim, a young man of about nineteen. He came with a heartbroken cry. His great desire was to be a missionary but, he said, "It's no use. I must give up the whole idea. I know my sins are forgiven, and I know I have a home in heaven. But, quite honestly, that isn't my biggest problem. It's nice to know my sins are gone, for that is all settled in Christ. It's good to know I have a home in heaven, but that may be years ahead. My big problem is not the past, or the future, but the present. Can Jesus Christ do anything for me now?"

He then went on to explain how the devil was bringing bitter and evil temptation to him. Even when he was in prayer and meditation, lustful and wicked thoughts, ideas, and pictures came into his mind. He told me how he had struggled to remove the foulness. He had made promises, prayed, and turned over new leaves, but nothing seemed to give him victory. In agony he cried, "Oh, how can I find deliverance from this sin?"

We prayed together and turned to God's Word for help and wisdom. First, I showed him that *temptation is not a sin*. That gave him some relief. (How the devil tries to crush the witness and steal the joy of Christians. If the devil can get us to believe that it is a sin to be tempted, then he has already won half the battle.) We looked at the temptations of our Lord, and saw how bitterly He was tempted—not three times only, as some would believe, but, as we read in Luke 4:13: "And when the devil had ended every [the complete cycle of] temptation, he [temporarily] left Him [that is, stood off from Him] until another more opportune and favorable time" (AMP). The devil was always seeking to tempt our Lord. We read in Hebrews 4:15 that He "was in all points tempted as we are, yet without sin." How important are the words, *in all points . . . yet without sin.*

Having learned that to be tempted is not in itself a sin, we turned then to the translation from Romans 5:10 (AMP), "*daily delivered from sin's dominion through His resurrection life.*" I explained to Jim that the very thing he longed for had already been provided. He could be daily delivered from sin's dominion, from the lustful temptations the devil brought to his mind. This deliverance came through the resurrection life of Christ. We considered the thoughts mentioned earlier in this chapter—that Jesus Christ lives in the believer in the Person and power of His Holy Spirit.

Jim's problem now was to find out how the indwelling Christ could help him overcome the temptations of the enemy. I suggested to Him that he should imagine that the center of his conscious mind was like a television screen. On this screen was flashed each thought and idea as it came to his attention. The form of the devil's attack was to flash on the screen lustful and impure thoughts and ideas. Even while Jim might be in prayer, on that screen came the attack of the enemy. Jim's attempts to remove the thoughts had only served to help bring them back again. By focusing his attention on them, he had linked them to his own thought sequence. The way to remove these temptations was not to grapple with them in deadly combat —that would only play into the hands of the devil. The sure way to win was to put something better and stronger in their place.

We then turned to the word of God and found the wonderful words in 1 Corinthians 15:57: "But thanks be to God, who gives us the victory through our Lord Jesus Christ." Here was the answer to Jim's problem— victory *now* through our Lord Jesus Christ. Every time the enemy swept in to attack, Jim was to say with conscious deliberation, "Thank You, Lord Jesus. You are my victory." It might require much repetition at first. He would have to stand firm and claim the victory in Christ.

That is what Jim did. I spoke to him at intervals over the following weeks and found out the result. He said that at first it was a hard fight, just claiming the victory, just saying "Thank You, Lord Jesus. You are my victory." It took maybe twenty or thirty repetitions to cleanse his "screen." As the days went by the victory came quicker because, very soon, the entrance of a foul thought immediately triggered off the prayer of victory.

What Jim was doing was putting into practice God's answer to all the dominion of sin. He was claiming a victory which had already been won, instead of fighting a battle which had already been lost.

This is the only successful answer to all the problems that come our way. We considered earlier in the chapter the glorious promise in 1 John 4:4, *"Greater is He that is in you than he that is in the world"* (KJV). The indwelling Christ is our armor. We saw, too, how so many Christians are limiting what God can do through them because of personal defeat in their own lives. This, above all else, is the weakness of the church today—the personal weakness and defeat of each member. If we could come, like Jim did, in all our weakness, and claim personal and daily victory —"Thank You, Lord Jesus, You are my victory"—what a different story it would be! The limiting of God would disappear as the reality of the indwelling presence and power of Christ was manifested.

Someone may say, "Yes, but I don't get temptations like Jim did. I'm older and the lusts of the flesh are not so strong." The thing to realize is that sin is not only vileness of the flesh in drunkenness and sexuality. The most searching definition of sin is found in Romans 14:23: "for whatsoever is not of faith is sin."

Whatsoever is not of faith—this is a searching phrase. The one who isn't attacked by lust will be sure to have other problems coming up against him. *Whatsoever is not of faith.* This puts care, fear, anxiety, and worry as weapons in the hand of the devil. How many Christians are snarled up by worry and anxiety! If we could only realize that we can be daily delivered from this kind of dominion, how much more joyous our lives would be! The Word of God is firm and sure that we can be daily delivered from sin's dominion by Christ's resurrection life.

I wonder if these words are being read by an anxious mother who doesn't know where to turn. God's salvation has a present tense for you. You can be delivered, moment-by-moment, if you will claim the victory of Christ. Dare you put Him to the test and cry in all sincerity, "Thank You, Lord Jesus. You are my Victory. You are my Peace"? It is for you He has promised, "I will never leave you nor forsake you." Why not claim a victory which has already been won instead of fighting the battle which you know is lost, even before you begin?

Are these words being read by a man who is plagued with the problems of business? Whether it is success or failure, each brings a tension that stretches out the nerves in a fever of spontaneous anxiety. Is your physical health beginning to suffer? Is your family life beginning to crack? Is your church life a burden? There is sure peace for you in the present tense of God's salvation. In spite of all you have done and cannot do, "Greater is He that is in you than he that is in the world." If you would only relate your problems to the victorious Christ; if you would take all that He is for all that you need, you could move into a present-tense experience of the peace of God that passes all understanding. Quit the fight and claim the victory.

Much of my work has been with teenagers and young adults. It is heartbreaking at times to see those who could be wonderful weapons in the hands of God lying idle and tied up with personal failure and present defeat. I wonder, are these words being read by some young woman or young man? You have trusted Christ as your Savior, and you know you are saved. But, like Jim, you are paralyzed by repeated failure, and desperate because of defeat in your personal life. Is it any comfort to you to know that you are not the only one in such a plight?

There are hundreds of young men and women who are limiting God because of personal defeat in their lives.

Many young people have an area in their lives where they know nothing but failure. Many a young man or woman is defeated by a secret habit of thought or word or deed. No one knows but you; you dare not tell anyone. How hard you have struggled and fought against it! Perhaps you started to play with sin some time ago, but now you are caught in its power. The whole thought of this acts as a sickening drag on your own personal life in Christ. There is so much more you want to do, but because of your secret sin you wouldn't dare. Suppose they found you out—you would never show your face again! There are hundreds of young men and women who are limiting God because of personal defeat in their lives. The devil knows it, and he wants to keep you there. He has lost you from his kingdom. Now if he can paralyze your witness for Christ, he will have neutralized your effectiveness as a child of God.

Why don't you stand in the armor of God? Get on your knees, first of all, before your Savior. Tell Him all the story of miserable defeat. Turn from your failure. Trust in Christ for a present tense salvation, then claim the victory that Christ has already won for you. "Thank You, Lord Jesus. You are my Victory." Keep on thanking Him for it. Dare to take Him at His word. Go on to grow strong in the Lord of Hosts, and in His mighty power. Prove to the devil and yourself that "greater is He that is in you than he that is in the world." Stop fighting a battle which has already been lost, and go on to claim the victory which has already been won—His Victory. Make it yours.

Paul says in Romans 7:18: "For I know that in me (that is, in my flesh,) nothing good dwells." In 2 Timothy 1:12 he cries: "I know whom I have believed and am persuaded that He is able to keep what I have committed to Him until that day."

Two things he knew—first, his own utter degradation; secondly, the overwhelming supremacy of the One to whom he had committed all. Thus he affirms in Philippians 4:13: "I can do all things through Christ who strengthens me." The Amplified Bible says it this way: "I have strength for all things in Christ Who empowers me [I am ready for anything and equal to anything through Him Who infuses inner strength into me; I am self-sufficient in Christ's sufficiency]."

Does that make you hungry for such an experience? And yet what did Paul have that you don't? Paul had Christ indwelling him, and so have you. The great difference is that in Paul, Christ had a willing weapon. God wasn't limited in Paul. He need not be limited in your life if only you will commit to Him every area of your personality. Paul said that Jesus Christ was "able to keep that which I have committed unto him." He keeps what I commit—it is as simple as that. *He keeps what I commit.* If I will commit to Him every area of my life, my areas of defeat as well as my areas of success, then He can move in and live through me.

God wasn't limited in Paul. He need not be limited in your life if only you will commit to Him every area of your personality.

Some of us hide our shame. We feel that Jesus Christ could never use such an abject failure as we are. We long for a greater experience of effectiveness in His service, but one glance at our life is sufficient to discourage us. We gaze on our areas of shame and failure, we hang our heads in sorrow—and we limit God. Listen again to Paul speaking: *"I have strength for all things in Christ who empowers me."* You, too, can claim that strength to conquer in the place of defeat. The strength is in Christ who can empower you. Go forward in faith, claiming the victory. Say, "Lord Jesus, this is my area of defeat, this is my place of shame (declare it openly to your Lord). Now, O blessed Master, I commit this to You. I commit my failure, my struggles, my tears. I claim Your victory. I believe that You have won the victory; therefore, I claim Your victory. Thank You, Lord Jesus. You *are* my victory!"

Live in the power of the present tense of your salvation: "daily delivered from sin's dominion by His resurrection life."

A further meaning to Paul's statement in Philippians 4:13 is, "I am ready for anything and equal to anything through Him Who infuses inner strength into me." When you have claimed the victory and proved the victory in your place of defeat, then you, too, can go on to say, "I am ready for anything and equal to anything, through Him Who infuses inner strength into me." Like blind Bartimeus, you can throw away your garment (your rags of shameful defeat), and go on to be a weapon in the hands of God. You will cease to limit God because you will be completely available and utterly expendable in His hands.

Before Paul could go on to do all things through Christ, he had to see his own utter failure, ruin, and degradation. He had to see it, to acknowledge it, and then to turn from it. Freely admitting that he had not one shred of goodness, he turned from all his failure to all the sufficiency of Christ.

In your life and my life, this twofold act is essential for blessing. We, too, must recognize the utter worthlessness of our fallen human nature. Then we must turn from it to receive the fullness of the indwelling Christ—"all that He is for all that I need."

3

Limiting God Through Selfishness

If we read Psalm 78 again, we find two other things standing out clearly. All the way through the psalm we meet the loving kindness of God to His people. The goodness of God is revealed again and again. Verse 4 recalls the praises of the Lord—His strength, His wonderful works. Verse 12 introduces the marvelous things He did "in the sight of their fathers." Then the psalmist lists them. He divided the sea. He split the rocks in the wilderness. He brought streams out of the rock. He rained down manna to eat. He rained flesh upon them like the dust. He, being full of compassion, forgave their iniquity. The psalm closes with these lovely words, "So He shepherded them according to the integrity of His heart, and guided them by the skillfulness of His hands." The whole psalm is a graphic record of the goodness of God poured out upon His people.

Over against this grace of God is recorded the mean ingratitude of those He had redeemed. The psalmist lists their behavior starting with verse 10. They did not keep the covenant of God, and refused to walk in His law. They forgot His works. They spoke against God. They said, "Can God prepare a table in the wilderness? . . . Can He give bread also? Can He provide meat for His people? . . . In spite of this they still sinned, and did not believe in His wondrous works."

Verses 34 and 36 show how double-hearted they were: "When He slew them, then they sought Him; and they returned and sought earnestly for God. . . . Nevertheless they flattered Him with their mouth, and they lied to Him with their tongue."

The utter selfishness and meanness of the people comes to us almost as a physical blow. God gave them nothing but love, and they spurned the hand that fed them. Even their seeming words of thanks were only flattery and lies. How our spirits rise in condemnation of such ingratitude.

But let us look at the way these people behaved in the light of 1 Corinthians 10, and perhaps we will see types of our own behavior. As we take these words to our hearts, each of us is bound to see the pointing finger, and to hear the solemn words, "Thou art the man."

Our Inheritance, His Inheritance

In Ephesians 1:10 we are introduced to the great and wonderful person of Christ, and in verse 11 we read that "we have obtained an inheritance" in Him. My inheritance *is* Jesus Christ. The very words open up the thought of the rich goodness of God towards us. Our sins have been cleansed in Christ's precious blood. We have been brought near to God in Him. We have been accepted by God in Him. Jesus Christ is my Redeemer, my Savior, my Advocate. He is the source of all the love and joy and peace in my life. All this we know, and all this we take.

But the other side of the picture is in verse 18: "the eyes of your understanding being enlightened; that you may know what is the hope of His calling, what are the riches of the glory of His inheritance in the saints." Here is Christ's inheritance in us. In other words, just as I cannot function without all that He is, so, in an amazing way, He cannot fulfill His true purposes without all that I am. We are His inheritance, His tools, His weapons, the vehicles He uses to implement His own will.

He created us, He redeemed us, we are not our own. But if the Lord needs us and calls for us, we reply, "Behold, here am I, send someone else."

At this point, perhaps, we can see ourselves in the types of Psalm 78. The children of Israel took all God offered. They asked for more, they expected more, they demanded more, and God gave freely for their needs. But God got very little in return. They were selfish, base, mean, and full of ingratitude. They limited God through their selfishness. Can this be true of some of us? Do we take so willingly all our inheritance in Christ? We expect to be blessed, comforted, and forgiven. We hold Him to His promises and say almost like Jacob in Genesis 32:26, "I will not let You go unless You bless me!" We demand our rights—and God honors His word and pours out His patient grace.

But if the Lord comes to us, and seeks for His inheritance in us—that is a different story. We don't mind taking all that He gives, but we are bitterly slow to respond to His request. He created us, and He redeemed us. We are not our own; He has bought us with a price—all this we agree to in principle. But if the Lord needs us and calls for us, we reply, "Behold, here am I, send someone else."

God is shamefully limited by the selfishness of His people. Every cent you own is His. Every second you live is His. Every breath you draw is in His hands. But in one way or another, we beg to be excused. We have just one short life in which we can serve Him before we spend an eternity enjoying the "much more" of our glorious inheritance in Him, only one short life to prove our love, to begin to respond to the agony of Olivet and the suffering of Calvary. But time and again we say, "I pray Thee, have me excused."

In our response to Christ, we are far worse than the children of Israel ever were in the desert. We withhold our finances, our fellowship, our fruitfulness—and God's work is limited. We talk about "my money," "my time," "my life," as if these were our prize possessions, as if we could do with them as we would.

There is a very searching word in Psalm 12:1—"Help, Lord, for the godly man ceases! For the faithful disappear from among the sons of men." How crisp is the phrasing, *the ceasing of the godly, the disappearance of the faithful*. Usually the psalmist deals with the harm done by the wicked in their opposition to the ungodly, but here the cry is against the godly and the faithful. Those who were godly are now ceasing; those who were faithful are now disappearing.

Verse 4 of the same psalm tells us why the godly are ceasing and the faithful failing: "Who have said, 'With our tongue we will prevail; Our lips are our own;

Who is lord over us?'" How modern is their reply, "My lips are my own, who is Lord over me?" People say today, "My time is my own, my money is my own, who is going to tell me what to do?" This is the selfishness that limits God—when the child of God denies to Jesus Christ the inheritance for which He died.

This is the selfishness that limits God— when the child of God denies to Jesus Christ the inheritance for which He died.

We read in Hebrews 12:2 that Jesus Christ "for the joy that was set before Him endured the cross, despising the shame." Part of that joy was His inheritance in the saints, His inheritance in you and me. How pathetic to think that our response to the love of Calvary is the selfishness of a heart that keeps back what it doesn't possess, and holds on to what belongs to another.

No Room In The Inn

As I am writing this now, it is Christmas Eve. Everywhere are the sights and sounds of Christmas. If we forget the commercialization of the festival for a moment, there still remains so much that is lovely and precious. The sweet fragrance of Christmas can still be felt within the hearts of faithful believers. The message of Christmas is being sung again—"Glory to God in the highest, and on earth, peace." These are the two things the coming of Christ effected—glory to God and peace on earth.

There can be no doubt that the coming of Christ brought glory to God. The angels said it would. The Father openly declared His good pleasure in His Son. The Lord Himself in John 17:4 pronounced the fact, "I have glorified Thee on the earth." These words, coming at the end of the earthly life that started in Bethlehem, give a full and authentic verdict—"I have glorified You on the earth."

There is no doubt of the glory—but to talk of peace on earth is another matter entirely. With the world in such turmoil, the idea of peace on earth seems a sheer impossibility. The cruel, cold facts reported daily by newspapers, television, and radio sicken the hearts of all who long for peace. Descending from the international level, through the national, through the domestic and family level, to the individual, the absence of peace everywhere is a stark reality. We are told that the ordinary man and woman of every country, every race, longs for one thing only—peace. But the peace so desired seems farther away than ever this Christmas.

Does this mean that Jesus has failed, that while He could produce the glory, He couldn't produce the peace? No, the answer is still the same as it was in Bethlehem, *"There was no room for them in the inn."* There is still no room for a Savior Who is Christ the Lord. There is room for a teacher, for a heroic example, for a pattern man, for all the other humanist descriptions applied to the Babe. But to *a Savior Who is Christ the Lord*, the world still closes its doors. In this way, the world today is limiting God. By locking the door against the Prince of Peace, the fact of peace is locked out also.

The boastful ones may try to persuade themselves that they have peace, like the man in Deuteronomy

29:19, who "blesses himself in his heart, saying, 'I shall have peace, even though I follow the dictates of my heart'—as though the drunkard could be included with the sober." What a pathetic attitude—he refuses the blessing of God and blesses himself! He assures himself that he will have peace in spite of selfishness and drunkenness. This is the world in which many an unbeliever is living today, a fantastic world built in the imagination, based on the blessing of a drunkard! No wonder God is shut out and limited.

The finest advertisement God has is a life which is full of peace despite the presence of sorrow, suffering, and want.

But there is a vital message here for the child of God. Many Christians have no real peace of heart, in spite of the fact that the Lord Jesus came to bring peace. Here again is where the limiting of God is seen. Because these Christians have no real peace themselves, they cannot be the blessing they ought to be. Because God is limited for them, He is limited through them. The finest advertisement God has is a life which is full of peace despite the presence of sorrow, suffering, and want.

We have been thinking of how we limit God through selfishness. Selfishness always produces an absence of peace. Show me a person who is enjoying the real, deep peace of God, and you will be showing me someone who is unselfish in thought and word and deed.

At Bethlehem the only place offered was a manger, away from the inn and the fellowship of men. Because they put Him in the manger, nobody in the inn was disturbed or put out of his own room. Everyone carried on as before. Because they put Him in the manger, nobody saw Him, except those who came seeking Him. The story of the manger makes a very pretty picture; it can be made to look so lovely and artistic. It may be a lovely picture, but it is a very poor practice. The story of the manger is repeated in many Christian hearts. They have heard the Gospel, the call of God to receive the Lord Jesus. They have opened their hearts to receive Him, but there has been no room in the inn. He has been guided to the manger of the heart, to the outside place.

It is so easy to invite the Lord in and put Him in the manger. There, just as at Bethlehem, no one in the inn is disturbed, nobody is put out of their room, everyone can carry on as before—"business as usual." If He is in the manger, no one in the inn will be annoyed, no complaints will be heard. Best of all, if He is in the manger, then no one will see Him. He will be on the premises, but not in possession; on the site, but not in sight. No wonder there is so little peace in many Christian hearts today! No wonder God is so terribly limited! Where there is no presence, there can be no power, no peace.

We saw in Ephesians 1:18 that the Lord Jesus has an inheritance in His people. He has an inheritance in you and in me, but it is not the manger of our hearts. The angel said to Zacharias in Luke 1:17 that his son-to-be would "make ready a people prepared for the Lord." That is exactly what true Christians should be, a people *prepared for the Lord*. The angel said to the shepherds in Luke 2:11, "For there is born to you this day in the city of David a Savior, who is Christ the Lord." The angels knew Him for who He really was—the Lord.

The wise men (Matthew 2) knew where to look for a king. They went to a palace to search for Him on a throne. But from there they were sent to an inn to search for a manger. A Lord or King does not live in a manger; he sits on a throne. You cannot rule from a stable. *You can only reign on a throne.* This seems so

---

There are many Christians who treat their spiritual life as a democracy. But Christianity isn't a democracy; it is a dictatorship! There is one Lord only: the Lord Jesus Christ.

---

obvious and simple, yet how many Christians have put the King in the manger! We in the United States do not believe in kings and lords. Our government is a so-called true democracy. The man who rules is an elected representative from the people. There are many Christians who treat their spiritual lives as a democracy. They have no kings or lords. The man in charge is an elected representative, and very often they themselves are the successful candidate. But Christianity isn't a democracy; it is a dictatorship!

There is one Lord only: the Lord Jesus Christ. If He is not Lord *of all* my life, then He is not Lord *at all* in my life. If He is in the manger, He cannot be on the throne. If Christ is in the manger, then God is limited.

Why do we repeat the Bethlehem story in our own lives, turning Him away from the inn and leaving Him in the manger? The answer is very simple—because of selfishness. If Christ is kept in the manger, it is because we do not wish to disturb the other guests in the inn. The inn of your heart is the place of everyday living, the place where people come and go and where all life's business is transacted. If the Lord came in to take possession, what a disturbance there would be!

Jesus Christ On The Throne

The human heart is composed of three parts. My mind, my emotions, and my will are the content of my heart or personality. In these three areas, the Lord seeks to rule from the throne. It is at this point that the costliness of the Christian life becomes the challenge to our innate selfishness.

John the Baptist's mission was to make ready a people prepared for the Lord. When we bring this message to our own hearts, we have many decisions to face. If Jesus Christ is to be Lord of my mind, then my mind must be prepared to receive Him. My thinking processes must be pure and holy. Some of the books I possess may need destroying.

This is what happened in Acts 19:18-19: "And many who had believed came confessing and telling their deeds. Also, many of those who had practiced magic brought their books together and burned them in the sight of all. And they counted up the value of them, and it totaled fifty thousand pieces of silver." The first thing these people did when they became Christians was to clean up their libraries. It must have been a wonderful witness for all the townspeople to see over $9,000 worth of books going up in smoke!

There is a tremendous amount of debased literature published these days, some of which finds its way into Christian homes. Jesus Christ must be Lord of my library, and what is dirty or doubtful or drivel should be burned—not given away! It might prove a costly bonfire, but it will help to prepare my mind for the Lord.

If we are not pure in mind, we cannot be pure in heart; and if we are not pure in heart, we cannot see God.

We may need to apply 2 Corinthians 10:5 to our minds: "casting down arguments and every high thing that exalts itself against the knowledge of God, bringing every thought into captivity to the obedience of Christ." Some of our imaginations and ambitions may need to be cast down. How searching, too, is the idea of bringing into captivity every thought to the obedience of Christ—to consider, as it were, the Lord Jesus, in the Person and power of His Holy Spirit, examining and censoring every thought that comes into my mind. This will most certainly prepare my mind for the incoming of the Holy and Just One. Purity of mind is not a highly prized possession today. Yet, if we are not pure in mind, we cannot be pure in heart; and if we are not pure in heart, we cannot see God. Certainly if Jesus Christ leaves the manger of my mind to move into the inn, many of the guests and inmates will be disturbed by His presence and will have to go.

If Jesus Christ is to be Lord of my heart, then He must be Lord also of my emotions and affections. It is here that the outward presence of the indwelling Lord should be most demonstrated. My emotions and reactions are many and varied, almost like the keyboard of a piano. From the deep base of bitter anger to a sweet treble of tender love, I express my reactions to the incidents in my life. But if Jesus Christ were Lord of my emotional life, and sat at the keys, many of my "recital pieces" would remain unplayed. If He were to initiate my reactions to the incidents of life, how different my behavior would be! There would be no sudden outbursts of rage or childish temper, no petty jealousy, no mean thoughts or vicious backbiting, no fawning flattery seeking personal advancement. There would be a purity and a holy quality about my emotions that would be outstanding. It would be on this emotional level that the presence of Christ on the throne would be first noticed.

You see, everyone with whom you relate in thought, word, or deed is aware of your emotional attitude toward them. If you are ruling your own life, then you will display your emotions at your own pleasure. Some of your contacts will feel your love and kindness, others will be disregarded, others will incur your anger or displeasure. You will react as you choose, for your own purposes, regardless of the implications. There will develop a pattern of reaction that will be the emotional characteristic of your personality, and everyone will recognize you from that emotional reaction.

But if Christ is given His inheritance in your emotional life, what a change will be seen! First and foremost, He will have an opportunity to display

Himself, and in this will be implemented the purpose of your redemption. He will be incarnate in you, and thus He will be able to carry on His ancient work of bringing love, hope, and comfort to the needy, the hopeless and the lost. As the Lord Jesus is given the control of your emotions, so your whole character will change. People will notice that something has happened to you. Jesus Christ won't be angry with anyone

---

Christ on the throne of your emotions is the answer to all life's fears. If you do not yield the throne, it is because you think either He cannot or will not cope with the situation.

---

who hurts you—He will say, "Father, forgive them." He won't be bitter against insult, nor will He retaliate when abused. He will not be fearful in danger, nor panic in sudden fear. He won't be consumed with anxiety, nor torn with frustration. He will be the peace of God in your heart, as you learn to say, "Lord Jesus, I am resting in You. I am leaving this to You. I am counting on Your promises that never fail." As you say this, and then do what you say, the peace of God will fill your heart.

Christ on the throne of your emotions is the answer to all life's fears. If you do not yield the throne, it is because you think either He cannot or will not cope with the situation. "Your Christ" is too small or too distant—yet all the time He lives in your heart and has said, "All authority has been given to Me in heaven and in earth. . . . and, lo, I am with you always,

even unto the end of the age" (Matthew 28:18,20).
Thus there will be seen in you a gradual change of
temperament. People will recognize it, wonder, and
ask why. All the time Christ will be magnified in you,
and His inheritance will be at His disposal.

How strange that what really satisfies Him will also
bring peace and joy to your heart. Over years of experience I have come to see that when Christ controls the
emotions, He also changes the character of the individual, because character is the pattern of behavior
resulting from continued emotional reaction. I have
also seen the Lord change a person's face. I have
watched hardness disappear as the love of Christ
begins to be displayed.

I was once speaking in Scotland when I met a lady
over eighty years of age. She looked like a real saint,
and she prayed like an angel. Her face was the picture
of loving devotion. Yet until she was fifty years old,
she had been a wicked woman. She told me herself
that she had been in jail over a hundred times for
drunkenness and disorder. Married at sixteen, she had
lived in sin, practicing every form of vice and wickedness. Then one day, in despair, after her husband had
hanged himself and her only son had been murdered
by his wife, she was on her way to put an end to
herself by flinging her broken body into the River
Clyde. She passed a building and heard the sounds of
hymn singing. As a last contact with the world, she
went in, sat down at the back, and listened. There God
spoke to her, and Christ met her need. That Sunday
night, thirty-seven years earlier, she had become a new
creature in Christ. Now she simply radiated Christ, in
thought and word and deed. She who used to display
Satan was now the one in whom Christ had full

control. Her face had been changed from lust to love, from wickedness to wonderful peace, from sin to serenity.

When Christ is on the throne of my emotions, I become the expression of His heart of love. As He daily expresses Himself through my emotions, the color of His presence is diffused throughout my being. His control is evident. His peace is solidly real. His work is my delight. Unconsciously, I will become more Christlike. I cannot help it, because His presence will cleanse, control, and conquer.

Paul said in Galatians 2:20: "I have been crucified with Christ; it is no longer I who live, but Christ lives in me; and the life which I now live in the flesh I live by faith in the Son of God, who loved me and gave Himself for me." We too may come to know the vital truth, "it is no longer I who live, but Christ lives in me"—in our emotions. There will be clarity of emotional response with an absence of mushy sentimentalism. It will be costly, but wonderfully satisfying. Even now as you read these words, the Holy Spirit may be putting His finger on the emotional strains and stresses in your life. Perhaps you have refused to ask forgiveness of someone you have offended, and have persisted in your pride. Remember that Christ humbled Himself in the days of His flesh, and if He is living in you, He still wants to humble Himself in the days of *your* flesh. You can always trust Him to do the right thing at the right time. Christ will never abuse your trust, but He will always be Himself. If He can claim His inheritance to the throne of your emotions, that sphere of limitation will vanish, and Christ will be exalted and glorified.

The third sphere where Christ seeks control is in the area of *my will*, the executive of my human personality. The mind reasons, the emotions react, and the will responds in an act of decision. The will is like the finger on the trigger. Once the will has responded, the decision is made and the trigger is squeezed. Often the will seems unreasonable, impetuous, and stupid. We blurt out a remark, then wish with all our hearts we had never said it. We decide on a course of action, and then spend months, sometimes years, in an agony of remorse. How often at a trial the accused sobs out, "I never meant to do it. I don't know what made me do it!" But it was done, and the act, the crime, the murder, was committed because of an uncontrolled act of the will. In the will, more than any other area of the human heart, the selfishness of man is displayed.

It sounds so obviously true to say, "I have a right to my own will!" That is what the world says and expects. But consider the words of the Son of God, He who was rich, by Whom all things were made:

> "My food is to do the will of Him who sent Me" (John 4:34).
> "I do not seek my own will but the will of the Father who sent Me" (John 5:30).
> "For I have come down from heaven, not to do My own will, but the will of Him who sent Me"(John 6:38).
> "O My Father, if it is possible, let this cup pass from Me; nevertheless, not as I will, but as You will" (Matthew 26:39).

He possessed all things, but He yielded His will to the One who had sent Him. Under no other conditions could He possibly have said, *"I always do those things that please Him"* (John 8:29).

In no other way can we give to God the pleasure He seeks. Only when He is allowed to overrule reason and guide in the area of my mind, to react to a given situation through the means of my emotions, and to respond by a decision which He has made—only then can Christ come into His inheritance in me. Only then can His life be lived out in terms of my humanity. Only then can I know that I am not limiting God through selfishness.

4

Limiting God Through Fear

In a previous chapter, we saw how the children of Israel limited God through fear when they turned back in the day of battle. But there is another kind of fear mentioned in Psalm 78 which is common today—the fear of indecision. This is the fear that holds back from ever setting out on the way to battle. Verse 8 says that the Israelites in the wilderness were "a generation that did not set its heart aright, and whose spirit was not faithful to God." Verse 37 says of them, "their heart was not steadfast with Him, nor were they faithful in His covenant." These verses give us the same two facts: their hearts were not set aright—that is, they were not properly prepared; they were not steadfast —that is, they were not faithful to God.

At the very outset of Israel's journey there was weakness. The whole field of future failure was the harvest of an unprepared heart. Their relationship with God was founded on an unprepared heart and faithless spirit. An old proverb says, "A good start is half the battle." There are some people in our churches who stand in a form of relationship to God without any means of being productive for His glory, because there never was a properly prepared heart.

We can see this thought better if we look at Romans 12:1-2: "I beseech you therefore, brethren, by the mercies of God, that you present your bodies a living sacrifice, holy, acceptable to God, which is your reasonable service. And do not be conformed to this world, but be transformed by the renewing of your mind, that you may prove what is that good and acceptable and perfect will of God."

"That good and acceptable and perfect will of God." Have you always found the will of God good? Have you always found the will of God acceptable? Have you always found it perfect? Many will say, "Decidedly not! Certainly not always good, definitely not always acceptable, and very often not always perfect, at least where I am concerned." This answer means that somehow we have missed out, because we are definitely expected to be able to prove all three characteristics of God's will—good, acceptable, and perfect. The reason we miss out is the same fault we saw in Psalm 78:8-9—we start our Christian life with an unprepared heart.

Present . . . That You May Prove

I have found it helpful to understand Romans 12:1-2, if I underline the word "present" in verse one and then connect it with a line to the words "that you may prove" in verse 2. The first kernel of truth is: *Present . . . that you may prove.* The reason so many of God's people complain about God's dealings with them, why so many find the will of God far from good, acceptable, and perfect, is that they would like to turn that sentence around. They would like to prove before they present. "If only God would show me His plan for my life," they say. "If only I knew what lies ahead!" But it doesn't work that way. We cannot first prove the will of God and then, if it is to our liking, go on to present our bodies to Him. God's order is *present . . . that you may prove.*

At this point the fear mentioned at the beginning of this chapter starts to operate. If our hearts are never properly prepared, we enter into the Christian pathway in a slap-happy way, giving easy assent to certain facts. It would almost seem, in many cases, that the decision to be a Christian was the end in itself. But the decision is not the end, only the means to an end.

We cannot first prove the will of God and then, if it is to our liking, go on to present our bodies to Him. God's order is present . . . that you may prove.

The next essential for proving God is a prepared heart and a faithful spirit—and this is where it hurts. If my heart is to be properly prepared for God, the truth of Romans 12:1 must first be real in my life. I must present my whole self as a "living sacrifice, holy, acceptable unto God." Many of God's people have by-passed that challenge. As they started on their pathway and came to this costly decision, it proved too big for them. They were afraid to face up to it. As a result, their lives only limit God. They are seeking to live the Christian life with an unprepared heart. This means that they have set themselves a pattern for all future behavior under similar circumstances. Whenever faced with the challenge of presenting all to

Christ, or with the costliness of the Christian life, they will have to hedge round it, wriggle out of it, and evade the issue at all costs.

Let us be perfectly honest about this. There are many Christians sitting in our churches at home who ought to be out on the foreign field. God has challenged them in days gone by, but they had already evaded the issue from the start. When they became children of God there came the call to "present your bodies," but they avoided facing up to their relationship to God. Their hearts were not properly prepared.

It is no secret that in this crazy world in which we live, the United States must always stay ready and prepared for an aggressor. There is the maximum amount of possible preparation so that not one second would be lost in an emergency. We pray that these forces may never be needed, but they are ready at a word of command to meet the aggressor.

"Maximum possible preparation"—that is how you and I ought to be in relation to God. Not that when faced with an opportunity of service for Him, we consider it and think about it then and there, but that we have a heart which has been properly prepared right from the start. We have faced Romans 12:1, and on our knees we have come to the only possible decision. From that moment we, too, are air-borne, fully prepared, awaiting only the word of command. The tragedy is that so many Christians have dodged the issue at the start. They never said "Yes," and they never said "No." There was just a hazy indecision which meant but one thing—an unprepared heart. So, as always, God was limited because they were unprepared.

Let us bring this verse into the open and face up to it, once and for all. "I beseech you therefore, brethren, by the mercies of God, that you present your bodies a living sacrifice, holy, acceptable to God, which is your reasonable service." We should first of all realize what it doesn't mean. To present my body a living sacrifice doesn't mean giving a little more to the offering in church. Nor does it mean going to church more often. Nor does it mean being a better man or woman. Neither does it mean going to Bible College, or to the mission field, or becoming a pastor, or a Christian worker. It means exactly what it says.

I must first of all consider the mercies of God to me—how good He has been to me, how He has saved me from a lost eternity, how He has made it possible for me, at the end of this very short earthly life, to be with Him in a place of perfection—a new heaven where there is no hunger, no separation, no pain, no sorrow, and no sin. This blessed place will be my home for eternity! How amazing are the mercies of God, when all the time I might have been left in my sin to go to a Christless eternity of separation from God. I should think on these things until, "by the mercies of God" and because of His everlasting goodness, I kneel before Him to say "thank you."

But my feeling of gratitude is such that words are not enough. Instead of speaking, I present myself to God. I present not only my time, my talents, but *my very self*, with words like this: "O Heavenly Father, my heart is full of gratitude for all Your goodness to me. I am only a poor wretched sinner, and yet You have made me Your child. You have received me into Your family and into Your everlasting Kingdom. Now, O God, I present myself as a living sacrifice to You, for

You to use, where and as You will. My heart is prepared, O God, my hands are off my life. I am ready, awaiting Your command. For Christ's sake. Amen."

If we are honest about the whole thing, this is the only possible decision to make. As Paul puts it, this is "your reasonable service." (How unreasonable some of us are!) Having made that decision, having presented our bodies in one solemn act of dedication, we may arise and go forward with a prepared heart. We are then in a position of permanent availability, so that God can call on us at any time, and under any circumstances. When the opportunity arises for witness or service, the question of what we should do need never arise. We have made a complete, once-for-all presentation of ourselves, and we expect God to take us at our word.

The sacrifice that I present to God—that is, my whole self—must have three characteristics. It must be living, holy, acceptable. If I have made this threefold sacrifice, then I will prove the will of God to be threefold—good, acceptable, perfect. The trinity of presentation brings a trinity of proof.

If my sacrifice, my presentation of myself, is living, alert, ready, and fully prepared, then the will of God will always be good to me. The mercy of God that gave me life will lead me always to expect nothing but good from such a Heavenly Father. Because I now live, He can be nothing but goodness to me.

If the presentation of myself to God is holy, then whatever His will may be, it will be acceptable to me. The word "holy" here means separate, set apart for God, and the word "acceptable" means well-pleasing. Thus if I am truly set apart for God and His purposes, whatever His will may be, it will be well-pleasing to me.

If my offering is acceptable, then I will find His will to be perfect. "Acceptable" again means well-pleasing, and "perfect" here means complete, with nothing missing. How appropriate this third part is then. If I am well-pleasing to God, His will will be complete; nothing will be missing. Thus, if I present myself, I will most surely prove His will to be good, well-pleasing, and complete. And so it will come to pass that my prepared heart, ready always to do His will, will never limit the purposes and counsels of God.

If I am truly set apart for God and His purposes, whatever His will may be, it will be well-pleasing to me.

Another truth we find in Romans 12:1-2 is that "presentation leads to transformation." As I present my body, living, holy, acceptable to God, the command then comes in verse 2, "And do not be conformed to this world, but be transformed." This transformation is not something I can do myself. I can only be transformed by the renewing of my mind—or as the Amplified Version says, "by the [entire] renewal of your mind [by its new ideals and its new attitude]." This is the cost of having a prepared heart.

A Faithful, Steadfast Spirit

The two verses we looked at from Psalm 78 at the beginning of this chapter, showed us that the children of Israel limited God because their hearts were not prepared, and because they were not steadfast or faithful to God. These two things are necessary for God's service—a prepared heart and a faithful spirit. We have seen the story of the prepared heart in Romans 12:1-2. There is still the need for a faithful, steadfast spirit.

This truth is wonderfully illustrated in the books of Ezra and Haggai. Ezra follows 2 Chronicles which ends with the utter destruction of Jerusalem by Nebuchadnezzar, and the city lying in waste for seventy years. 2 Chronicles 36:22 records how Cyrus, King of Persia, was moved by God to start the rebuilding of the house of God. This movement by God is also recorded in Ezra. It shows us the challenge coming to the Jews who were living in peace in the land of their captivity, where they had found prosperity. But there were those who, in the words of Romans 12:1, "presented their bodies a living sacrifice." With hearts truly prepared, they left all the comforts they had gathered, and tramped for months to the ruined city of Jerusalem. Here they found nothing but desolation, destruction, and weed-covered ruins. As they struggled on with their building, they encountered difficulties and opposition on every side. Their prepared hearts were being fully tested.

The book of Haggai also covers the same period. The whole of Haggai consists of thirty-eight verses in two small chapters, but it contains a message especially for the church today. It was written because somebody said one short sentence. This may sound strange, but it is perfectly true. The reason for the writing of Haggai is seen in chapter 1, verse 2: "This people says, 'The time has not come, the time that the LORD's house should be built.'" It is the story of "The Lost Vision," of people who once had a prepared heart, but who failed to have a faithful, steadfast spirit.

These former captives had left all for God. They had suffered much; they were heroes of the faith—but they limited God. Haggai's challenging word is "Consider your ways!" The only reason they had ever left their pleasant homes in the Empire of Persia, was to come with a prepared heart to build a house for God. So Haggai cries (verse 4), "Is it time for you yourselves to dwell in your paneled houses, and this temple to lie in ruins?"

The result of a lost vision is a life full of dissatisfaction—plenty of effort with little to show for it.

In verse 6 God shows them the results of the lost vision: "You have sown much, and bring in little; you eat, but do not have enough; you drink, but you are not filled with drink; you clothe yourselves, but no one is warm; and he who earns wages, earns wages to put into a bag with holes."

The result of a lost vision is a life full of dissatisfaction—plenty of effort with little to show for it. Here surely is the message for us today, a challenge to those who set out with a prepared heart, but who fail to remain true and steadfast to the original call. In so doing they limit God, in spite of a separated life.

It is interesting to see in the first chapter of Haggai the whole story of how God deals with those who have lost their vision. First there is the *reason*—they have said "the time has not come." Then came the *result* of the lost vision—much activity but little productivity. In verses 7 and 8 we find the *recall* and *reminder* from God:

"Thus says the LORD of hosts: 'Consider your ways! Go up to the mountains and bring wood and build the temple, that I may take pleasure in it and be glorified,' says the LORD."

The ultimate aim of all their work was that God should be glorified. As the Westminster catechism says, "Man's chief aim is to glorify God and to enjoy Him for ever."

Then comes the *repentance* of the people. In verse 12, we read that the rulers "with all the remnant of the people, obeyed the voice of the LORD their God." Finally comes the *return* of God to the midst of His people: "I *am* with you, says the LORD."

It is this message of Haggai which is so needed in our churches today. Apart from those who have never had a vision, and who have never presented their whole lives to God, there are many to whom God has spoken in past days.

Very often I counsel people who say with a weary heart, "You know, once the things of God meant everything to me. I had committed all to Him, and I was so busy and happy serving my Lord." Then they go on to tell how the vision faded, and their burning hearts grew cold. They got taken up with so many other "things"—not necessarily evil or wicked things, but things which absorbed their time, their money, and their lives. Eventually they found themselves saying "Yes, of course, the things of God are very important. Yes, I fully intend some day to put in an all-out effort—but not just now. I've got so many

other things all lined up, I can't really spare the time."
And so the vision fades as they lose their order of
priorities. They plunge into a busy world of "things"—
good things, honest things maybe, but still just things.
They had a prepared heart as had the builders of
Haggai's day, but they didn't have a faithful and
steadfast spirit.

I saw the opposite of this wonderfully illustrated in
a church I visited several years ago. I was speaking at
a midweek prayer meeting in the month of August,
and I went to the church expecting to find the faithful
few. By the time we began there were nearly three
hundred members there, and they all meant business!
There is a fine story behind this. The present pastor
had been there for about fifteen years. When he came
the membership was very small, and the impact of the
church on the world was practically nil. But the pastor
was, above all else, a man of vision with a wonderfully
prepared heart, and a very faithful, steadfast spirit.
The church had grown steadily in numbers and
vigorously in outlook, with a vision that extended far
and wide.

Some time before it had become obvious that the
present auditorium would soon be too small for the
increasing attendance. So schemes were discussed, and
plans were made and drawn for a new auditorium. The
architect's drawings were hanging in the entrance hall
when I went. I was much impressed. The money to
build had come in, and before long the building fund
was an impressive sight.

Then it was that the prepared heart and the
steadfast spirit took over the whole situation. The
vision of the church by now was an uplifted vision.
Their missionary program was alive, growing and

vigorous. When they viewed the needs of the mission field and then considered their own building fund, they made a tremendous decision. They decided not to spend their money on a vast rebuilding program. Instead, they installed closed circuit television in the large hall below, thus doubling their seating capacity. The large sum of money on hand was invested in the larger vision of the greater need elsewhere.

When I heard this story, my heart rejoiced. Here was no limitation of God, but the reverse. From this one church there radiates power and life and joy and blessing. Who can measure the untold honor and glory that has been added to the Lamb of God through the witness of this one church? It began almost as a modern counterpart of the book of Ezra. Men and women with prepared hearts came to rebuild a place of failure. They found destruction, opposition, and persecution, but there was also a continuing, faithful, steadfast spirit which had a glorious vision. This vision remains, enhanced, uplifted, outreaching, and God is at work, unlimited in His blessing.

Many churches, as bodies of believers, possess this same vision. They have recognized why they are called out, and they have maintained the vision steadfastly and faithfully. As a church they have "a prepared heart" and a "presented body" which is truly living, holy, and acceptable.

There is one other side of this truth which needs to be considered in connection with the story of Ezra and Haggai. Not only were the people called out as a body to rebuild the temple, but each one had his own individual responsibility to God.

In the same way, we personally have our own responsibility to God. When we consider 1 Corinthians 6:19-20, we can find a message for our own hearts today: "Or do you not know that your body is the temple of the Holy Spirit who is in you, whom you have from God, and you are not your own? For you were bought at a price; therefore glorify God in your body and in your spirit, which are God's. . . ."

The Purpose of His Coming

The ultimate purpose of the coming of Christ was to restore our true humanity. As He said in John 10:10, "I have come that they may have life, and that they may have it more abundantly." God's salvation is not merely the forgiveness of sins, but the restoration of life in the person of the Holy Spirit of Christ.

God's salvation is not merely the forgiveness of sins, but the restoration of life in the person of the Holy Spirit of Christ.

Psalm 69 is one of those precious psalms that speaks of the crucifixion of Christ, as verse 21 especially tells us: "They also gave me gall for my food, and for my thirst they gave me vinegar to drink." The last phrase of verse 4 contains a jewel of truth: ". . . *then I restored that which I took not away*" (KJV). Applying this to Christ's death, as He was dealing with the whole question of our salvation, He not only bore our sins in His own body on the tree, but He also dealt with the problems of *the restoration of life.*

This aspect of the work of Christ is sometimes overlooked, or almost ignored, in considering the great work of salvation. So often the emphasis is placed on the forgiveness of sins, as if that was the most important part of the work of Christ. John gives us the last word, as it were, on the purpose of the Gospel, in chapter 20, verses 30 and 31:

"And truly Jesus did many other signs in the presence of His disciples, which are not written in this book; but these are written that you may believe that Jesus is the Christ, the Son of God, and that believing you may have life in His name." That is the ultimate aim of the Gospel—*that you may have life in His name.*"

The phrase "in His name" is a literal rendering of the original, but it has little meaning for us in English. We read it only as words with no real inner significance—"in His name"—nor do the words make us stop and think. But in the Amplified Version the phrase (both here and in the other places) becomes alive— "through (in) His name [through who He is]." Now the whole phrase is charged with power—that you may have life through Who He is.

When we put this truth with verse 4 of Psalm 69, the inner meaning is revealed. *"Then I restored that which I took not away."* Jesus Christ restored life— spiritual life, eternal life—through what He is. In other words, the life He restored wasn't an item, a thing, an "it," but *Himself.* "I am the way, the truth, and the life," He said. He Himself was the life that He restored.

It is lovely to put that verse alongside John 1:29. "The next day John saw Jesus coming toward him, and said, 'Behold! The Lamb of God who takes away the sin of the world!'" We can now see again the twofold work of Christ. He took away that which He did not commit (our sin), and He restored that which He did not take away (our life).

That great text, John 3:16, has the same twofold idea: "For God so loved the world that He gave His only begotten Son, that whoever believes in Him should not perish (dealing with the sin question) but have everlasting life (dealing with the restoration of life)." 1 John 5:11-12 is dogmatic on this point:

"And this is the testimony: that God has given us eternal life, and this life is in His Son. He who has the Son has life; and he who does not have the Son of God does not have life."

John 3:16 shows both the negative side of my salvation (my sin dealt with) and the positive side (the restoration of life). So much weak and feeble Christian living comes from a negative appreciation of the work of Christ. The negative side was necessary, vitally necessary, but not as an end in itself. It was necessary that my sin should be dealt with, but only as a means of bringing me into a right relationship with God, in order that I might have *life by virtue of Who and what He is.*

Therefore when I read 1 Corinthians 6:19-20 and see that my body is the temple of the Holy Ghost, I realize that the One Who indwells me is the Lord Jesus in the Person of His Holy Spirit. Romans 8:9 is quite definite on this point: "Now if anyone does not have the Spirit of Christ, he is not His." Jesus Christ indwells by His Holy Spirit. The life has been restored, but has the temple been rebuilt? Our verse in Haggai 1:2 described those who said, "The time has not come, the time that the LORD's house should be built." You remember, the only reason they ever left their place of pleasurable captivity to go to a ruined and desolate area was to rebuild the Temple of God. They were doing this for *Him* to find pleasure and be glorified in it.

So it is with us. The ultimate purpose of our salvation is not that we should escape a coming judgment, but that we might live for His pleasure and to His glory. This is attained when the "temple is rebuilt." 1 Kings 8:60-61 records part of King Solomon's blessing of the people when the first earthly Temple was dedicated: "that all the peoples of the earth may know that the LORD is God; there is no other. Let your heart therefore be loyal to the LORD our God. . . ."

God replied to Solomon's consecration: "I have heard your prayer and your supplication that you have made before Me; I have consecrated this house which you have built to put My name there forever, and My eyes and My heart will be there perpetually" (1 Kings 9:3).

The ultimate purpose of our salvation is not that we should escape a coming judgment, but that we might live for His pleasure and to His glory.

When the Temple was properly completed and faithfully dedicated, God promised that His name, His eyes, and His heart would be there for ever. But to us God has given a more precious promise—not only His name, His eyes, and His heart, but *Himself*—God the Son, in the power of His Holy Spirit. The trinity of promise for Solomon becomes the Trinity of Persons for us. What was "His name" for Solomon's day is for us "God the Father." What was "His eyes" is for us "God the Holy Spirit." What was for Solomon "His heart" is for us "God the Son." May we realize the honor and the dignity which is ours in *being* the temple of God. With the men of Haggai's day, may we see and admit the failure and weakness in our lives.

"'You have sown much, and bring in little; you eat, but do not have enough; you drink, but you are not filled with drink; you clothe yourselves, but no one is warm; and he who earns wages, earns wages to put into a bag with holes. . . .' 'You looked for much, but indeed it came to little;' . . . 'Why?' says the LORD of hosts. 'Because of My house that is in ruins . . .'" (Haggai 1: 6-9).

A humble act of self-examination will show us that unless we rebuild a Temple that is holy and pure and for His glory, we can never know fruit that remains, feeding that really satisfies, fellowship that abides, and service that brings glory to God, grace to others, and eventually gladness to our own hearts.

If God is to be unlimited in our lives, then it will only be as He is unlimited in our daily living. Our body physically, mentally and morally must be prepared as a temple of God. *Holiness must not be only a word in a book; it must be interpreted into the fiber of our daily lives.* A holy temple is a Spirit-filled temple, which means an exalted Christ, and an unlimited God.

5

Limiting God Through Unbelief

If we will read Psalm 78 again, we will find another characteristic of the children of Israel which can be a warning to us. It is found in two verses: "Because they did not believe in God, and did not trust in His salvation" (vs. 22). "In spite of this they sinned still, and did not believe His wondrous works" (vs. 32).

This must surely seem very strange to us. The children of Israel had seen the hand of God at work in Egypt. They had been most wonderfully redeemed. Their needs had been met, and their wants supplied. Yet they did not believe God. It sounds fantastic that this should be so, but it was. In spite of all that God had done for them, they still questioned His ability and His purpose. "Can God prepare a table in the wilderness?" they asked (vs. 19). So they limited God through unbelief. *They had enough belief to get themselves out of Egypt, but not enough to get themselves into Canaan.* The promises of God were made, the assurance from God was given, and the wealth of Canaan was theirs the moment they left Egypt. But because of unbelief, they did not enter in, and God was limited through their unbelief.

Unbelief is characteristic of many of God's people, both in the Bible and in the church today. Jacob's life exemplifies the results of unbelief in the promises of God. In Genesis 27 we have recorded the story of the stolen blessing. Isaac, feeling his end was near, sent his favorite son Esau to the field to hunt for deer. Esau was to prepare venison for his father so that his father could eat and then bless him. Rebekah heard all this, so she instructed Jacob, Esau's twin and her favorite, to deceive Isaac so that *he* could acquire the blessing. The story is one long record of lies, deceit, and trickery. Jacob blatantly said he found the deer "because the LORD your God brought it to me"—what blasphemy! The story ends with the reader feeling very sorry for the villain, Esau, and utterly repulsed with the behavior of Jacob, the hero—because Jacob *was* God's man. It is in this story that Jacob lives up to the meaning of his name—deceiver, liar, twister.

The whole point of this miserable story is that it need never have happened. It was so unnecessary. It all came about because of Jacob's unbelief. God had already made His promise (Genesis 25:23). He had already said that the elder would serve the younger. He had already promised both the birthright and the blessing to Jacob. Rebekah knew all this because the promise was made to her at her request—she had inquired of the Lord (Genesis 25:22). Thus she knew the promises from the very beginning. Jacob was her favorite son, and no mother ever keeps back anything from her favorite son. Esau was the strong man, the man who could get things done, while Jacob was the weakling, the domestic type who liked to be about the house. But Rebekah must surely have comforted him with the knowledge that all was to be his, that he was to succeed his father Isaac.

Although Jacob knew the promises of God, he prepared his own plans to get what God had already promised—the perfect example of unbelief. He need never have lifted a finger, and both the birthright and the blessing would have come to him. God had promised it so. In God's own time, and in God's own way, all the promises for Jacob would have come true. *But Jacob couldn't wait.* He couldn't keep his hands off the promises of God. He planned, lied, schemed, and deceived to get what was already his.

Although Jacob knew the promises of God, he prepared his own plans to get what God had already promised—the perfect example of unbelief.

God had made promises, but Jacob had made his own plans. So Jacob had to pay the price for unbelief. Galatians 6:7 is true for all time and for all types: "Do not be deceived, God is not mocked; for whatever a man sows, that he will also reap." This verse contains a warning, a truth, and a law. The warning—"Do not be deceived." The truth—"God is not mocked." The law—"whatever a man sows, that he will also reap."

Jacob was deceived. He who was the arch deceiver was deceived by his own heart. Jacob mocked God. His very planning was proof of his disbelief, and disbelief is the height of mockery. Jacob was to reap a harvest through all his life because of his unbelief. As a result of his trickery, Esau swore to kill him. Rebekah, in her anxiety for her beloved son, said to him, "Arise, flee to my brother Laban in Haran. And stay with him a few days, until your brother's fury turns away" (Genesis 27:43-44). To save his life, Jacob left the home he loved and the mother he loved, for *"just a few days."* But listen to his voice crying out in distress in chapter 31:38: "These twenty years I have been with you." The few days turned into over twenty years. Over twenty years of separation from the home he loved and from the mother he adored! The price that Jacob paid for his unbelief was to lose the very thing he loved most—his home life.

Even when his own family came, and he had a home of his own, it was never a happy home, full of love and tenderness. His own children grew up to lie to him, to cheat him, and to deceive him. Jacob certainly reaped a hundredfold these seeds of deceit he sowed that day. And his experiences during those twenty years with Laban were utterly humiliating. He was tricked and deceived by both his uncle and his cousins. With no one to turn to, he must have felt the bitterness that he himself had put in the heart of Esau.

But the point is, it was so unnecessary. If only Jacob had believed God, and rested on the promises of God, all the goodness would have been his without the grief. But no—God promised, Jacob planned, and then he paid the bitter price of unbelief. Just as the children of Israel limited God by their unbelief, so the plans of Jacob limited the fullness of joy that might have been his.

God Promises, Abraham Plans

Another great character in whose life we can learn the same lesson is Abraham. In Genesis 13 we read that after Lot had made his choice to go to the well-watered plain of Jordan, God made a promise to Abram. (His name had not yet been changed to Abraham.)

"And the LORD said unto Abram, after Lot had separated from him: 'Lift your eyes now and look . . . for all the land which you see I will give to you and your descendants forever'" (Genesis 13:14-15).

There was the beginning of the promise—a son for Abraham. Sometime later the whole matter was raised again. Abraham asked God (in chapter 15:2), "Lord GOD, what will You give me, seeing I go childless. . . ?" God promised him, in verse 4, a son out of his own body, and a succession of seed as many as the stars of heaven. Verse 6 distinctly says that Abraham "believed in the LORD, and He accounted it to him for righteousness." Paul makes much of the faith of Abraham in Romans 4, even quoting Genesis 15:6: "For what does the Scripture say? *'Abraham believed God, and it was accounted to him for righteousness'*" (vs. 3).

Abraham is indeed the father of the faithful, but he wasn't always so. There was a time when, like his grandson Jacob, he heard the promises of God and believed them, but then went on to make his own plans. Genesis 16 contains this story of the unbelief of the believer.

After God had renewed his promise in Genesis 15, Abraham waited for the son to come. He waited one year, two years, three, four . . . ten years—but no son came. So it was that he took a hand in the matter and planned to get what God had already promised. He had only to await God's time, but that proved to be too long. Chapter 16 begins: "Now Sarai, Abram's wife, had borne him no children. And she had an Egyptian maidservant whose name was Hagar. So

Sarai said to Abram, 'See now, the LORD has restrained me from bearing children. Please, go in to my maid; perhaps I shall obtain children by her.' And Abram heeded the voice of Sarai. Then Sarai, Abram's wife, took Hagar her maid, the Egyptian, and gave her to her husband Abram to be his wife, after Abram had dwelt ten years in the land of Canaan."

So Abraham married Hagar. Immediately Hagar conceived, and a child was born—a son! Abraham had planned and gotten what God had already promised. But just as in Jacob's case, where God had promised and Abraham planned, a price had to be paid. Abraham sowed, but he had also to reap.

Where God had promised and Abraham planned, a price had to be paid. Abraham sowed, but he had also to reap.

The first thing was a breakdown of family relationships. Sarah was despised by her maid, and in her bitter reaction Abraham was left with two wives in opposition to each other. Domestic happiness was gone. Then God gave His verdict on Abraham's plan. He said of the son to be born, "He shall be a wild man; His hand shall be against every man, and every man's hand against him" (16:12). Imagine peaceful Abraham having a son who would be a wild man. But then, Ishmael wasn't the son of God's promise, but of Abraham's plan!

Genesis 21 tells us of the fulfillment of God's promise: "And the LORD visited Sarah as He had said, and the LORD did for Sarah as He had spoken. For

Sarah conceived and bore Abraham a son in his old age, at the set time of which God had spoken to him." Ishmael was fourteen years old when Isaac was born. Abraham had to wait not ten years, but twenty-four years! But it all came true as God had promised.

This isn't the end of the story, however, because there was still Ishmael, the wild man whose hand was to be raised against every man and every man's hand against him. He wasn't God's promise, but see how Abraham loved him: "And Abraham said to God, 'Oh, that Ishmael might live before You!'" (17:18). Abraham wanted God to support his plan, so that Ishmael might become the child of promise. He had schemed to produce a son, but Ishmael wasn't the son who would inherit. In fact, a simple Bible study will show us what happened to the descendants of Ishmael.

In Genesis 37 we have the story of Joseph, God's man. In this story he is taken captive to Egypt. Who was it who took him down to Egypt? The Ishmaelites! The descendants of "Abraham's plan" took a son of "God's promise" down to Egypt as a captive. How amazing! Little did Abraham realize what his plan would lead to.

If we look at Psalm 83 we come to a series of verses that are both fact and prophecy. The psalm begins with a call for help. The enemies of Israel are scheming and combining against God's people: "They have said, 'Come, and let us cut them off from being a nation, that the name of Israel may be remembered no more.' For they have consulted together with one consent; they form a confederacy against You: the tents of Edom and the Ishmaelites" (vs. 4-6).

In the days of the psalmist, the Ishmaelites were scheming and combining with others to wipe out

Israel. Now the descendants of "Abraham's plan" were fighting against the whole people of Israel—open persecution.

But the most amazing thing about this psalm is its prophecy which is being fulfilled even in our day. Today there is a Kingdom of Israel once more. And Israel has a set of avowed enemies—the followers of Islam, the descendants of Ishmael!

So we have the fantastic fact that, humanly speaking, Abraham's plan is at the root of all the trouble in the Middle East. Ishmael is still at war with Isaac. What a price has been paid throughout all the years of struggle between Abraham's plan and God's promise. First it was against the man Joseph. Then it was against the people of Israel. Now it is against the whole nation. There is trouble now, not with a man, nor a people, but with the whole of the Middle East.

God made a promise to Abraham, to Jacob, and to the Jews in Egypt. In each case the promise was accepted, but it was never properly received. There was always that undercurrent of unbelief—the unbelief of the believer. In all this, God was limited—through unbelief.

God Promises, We Plan

1 Corinthians 10 tells us that as we read these stories, we will find types of our own behavior. So let us take warning. For, if God so dealt with His people the Jews, if they had a price to pay and a harvest to reap, how much more will this be true of us? Has God made any promises to us that might compare in magnitude with those to His people of old? If we look at 2 Peter 1:4, we find that God has "given to us

exceedingly great and precious promises." Notice the unique choice of language. These are not just *promises*, not merely *precious promises*, but *exceedingly great and precious promises*.

The Word of God uses a trinity of superlatives to describe the amazing quality of promises given to us. Such promises must be unique, and so they are. Verse 4 goes on to say, "that through these you may be partakers of the divine nature." I must confess that when I first saw these words and considered them, I felt as if the thought was somewhat blasphemous. That I should be made a partaker of God's nature sounds utterly preposterous. I have one nature already, a fallen human nature which is always prone to sin. But now the Word of God teaches that I can be a partaker of another nature: the divine nature.

When I consider this against the background of other Scriptures, however, I can understand more fully what is being taught. 1 John 5:11-12 tells me plainly, "that God has given us eternal life, and this life is in His Son. He who has the Son has life; and he who does not have the Son of God does not have life." 1 John 4:4 says, "You are of God . . . because He who is in you is greater than he who is in the world." The Amplified Version has a delightful translation of 1 John 3:24: "All who keep His commandments (who obey His orders and follow His plan, live and continue to live, to stay and) abide in Him, and He in them. [They let Christ be a home to them and they are the home of Christ.] And by this we know *and* understand *and* have the proof that He [really] lives *and* makes His home in us: by the (Holy) Spirit Whom He has given us."

So then, I really *am* a partaker of the divine nature. Jesus Christ lives in me in the Person of His Holy Spirit. I have life, and life isn't an "it," but a Person. Jesus told Thomas, "I am the way, the truth, and the life. No man comes to the Father except through Me" (John 14:6). Jesus *is* the Life, and He lives in me—this is the exceeding great and precious promise.

Jesus Christ lives in me in the Person of His Holy Spirit. I have life, and life isn't an "it" but a Person.

What does this promise offer me? To Abraham, the promise was a son. To Jacob, the promise was the birthright and the blessing. To the Jews from Egypt, the promise was Canaan. The promises were given, but they were not taken up as they should have been. The result was a harvest of sorrow for the individual, and a deliberate limitation of God. Could you be guilty of planning to get by your own efforts that which is yours by divine promise?

The Amplified Version of 1 John 5:18 may be able to help us on this point: "We know [absolutely] that anyone born of God does not [deliberately and knowingly] practice committing sin, but the One Who was begotten of God carefully watches over *and* protects him [Christ's divine presence within him preserves him against the evil], and the wicked one does not lay hold (get a grip) on him *or* touch [him]." (AMP)

This verse points to a high and holy quality of living, the very thing the Christian church needs today. It suggests that there is a life to be lived which is sparkling in its purity, the kind of life that unconsciously challenges the normal drab grays of other lives. This life can be mine *right now*, the promise says. I *am* a partaker of the divine nature, and Christ's divine presence within me preserves me against the evil.

All this we believe in a hazy, theoretical way—just as Abraham and Jacob believed. But like them, we start to make plans of our own. We determine that our lives shall be improved, and we work out our own plans for doing so. We turn over new leaves, we pray more, read more, try new gimmicks on holiness. In short, we do all we can to make our fallen human nature acceptable to God. Paul, however, could say in Romans 7:18, "For I know that in me (that is, in my flesh) nothing good dwells." But we don't go as far as that. We like to say, "Well, I know I'm not perfect. I do many things I shouldn't do. But, after all, there are some good points about me." Paul could say *no good thing* about himself apart from God. He told the Ephesians that before they were Christians they were *dead in trespasses and sins* (2:1), and he included himself in that description (2:5). That is why he could say in Galatians 2:20, "I have been crucified with Christ; it is no longer I who live, but Christ lives in me; and the *life* which I now live in the flesh I live by faith in the Son of God, who loved me and gave Himself for me."

Spiritually, Paul was dead and corrupt. The only life in him was the life of Christ. So many Christians slip up on this point. They think that Christ came to change our deadness into a new quality of life so that we can now struggle on with this patched-up human nature. They act as though our fallen human nature has been magically restored to life so that now we can do what we couldn't do before. It is at this point that we plan and scheme to get what God has promised. We know that God has promised joy and peace through victory over sin, and this we try to achieve with our patched-up human nature.

The epistle to the Colossians was written to true Christians. Yet in chapter 3, Paul tells them, "For you died, and your life is hidden with Christ in God. When Christ *who is* our life appears, then you also will appear with Him in glory" (vs. 3-4).

We seek to produce by our own efforts that quality of life that God has promised. The price we pay is frustration, bitter disappointment, decreasing effort, and a lowering of our standards.

Paul told the Ephesians they *were* dead before they became true Christians (2:1). He told the Colossians, "You *are* dead"—you are still dead, your human nature is still corrupt, sinful, and no good (3:3,4). The only life in you is Christ. In John 14:6 Jesus said that He is the life. He also said, "Because I live, you will live also" (John 14:19). The only possibility of my living is when Jesus comes to live His life in me. *God's promise was not a patch-up, but a Person.*

This is where we fall into the error of Abraham and Jacob. We recognize the need for a higher quality of living, and in spite of God's promise, we seek to produce by our own efforts that quality of life that God has promised. The price we pay is frustration, bitter disappointment, decreasing effort, and a lowering of our standards. For if we cannot reach the standards we have set, then we must lower our standards of living until we can meet them. No, we must accept this *exceedingly great and precious promise*. In humbleness and true confession we must admit our utter ruin, deadness, and loss. Then we must embrace the glorious truth that, although I am written off as a failure, there now lives in me One Who is my life. I can come to a place where the truth of Philippians 4:13 begins to dawn in my heart, "I can do all things through Christ who strengthens me." As we saw earlier in chapter 2, the Amplified Version says, "I have strength for all things in Christ Who empowers me [I am ready for anything and equal to anything through Him Who infuses inner strength into me; I am self-sufficient in Christ's sufficiency]."

Strength For All Things

The great challenge is whether we will admit the utter worthlessness of our fallen human nature and own up to our total spiritual deadness and bankruptcy. It will be helpful to recall that the Word of God records three cases where Christ raised the dead to life. One was Lazarus, whose deadness was utter corruption and with whom there was nothing pleasant or lovely. Another was the son of the widow of Nain. His body was cold and dead, though no corruption was as yet evident. The third was the daughter Jairus. She had just died, her body was warm, and there was still a loveliness about her form and features—but she was truly dead. Each of the three had a different outward appearance—utter corruption, cold stiffness, warm loveliness—but they were all dead. All three needed one thing: physical life.

Physical death is not always horrible and repulsive at first, but it soon leads to complete and utter corruption. There is only one answer to death, and that is life. No material benefits or rewards, no earthly honors or glories can meet the need—only life. The same is true of spiritual death. This was why Christ said to religious people, "I have come that they may have life, and that they may have *it* more abundantly" (John 10:10). The people to whom He spoke had the purest religion in the world, the finest laws ever written, the richest teachings from the lips of the blessed Lord Himself—but they were still spiritually dead. He came that they might have life. Notice He didn't say that they might live, but that they might *have life.* In other words, into their hearts, alongside their spiritually dead human nature, would come *life* in the person of His Holy Spirit.

So it is in your life and mine. When we become true Christians, we are born again. We receive life. This life is the presence of Christ in the person of His Holy Spirit. It is in this way that I become a partaker of the divine nature. But the essential point is that when He comes to be my life, He is the only Life I have. He is my *only* source of power, joy, peace, and victory. All *I* can do is fail, as I have proved all through my life. All *He* can do is succeed, as He has proved all through His life.

With this truth firmly in our hearts, let us look once more at some of the verses quoted above. We've already looked at 1 John 5:18 in the Amplified Version, but it bears repeating: "We know [absolutely] that anyone born of God does not [deliberately and knowingly] practice committing sin, but the One Who was begotten of God carefully watches over *and* protects him [Christ's divine presence within him preserves him against the evil], and the wicked one does not lay hold (get a grip) on him *or* touch [him]."

I can know a peace and a joy through victory over sin, but I am not gaining the victory. The victory comes as I recognize first, my utter helplessness to succeed, and second, that Christ's divine peace within me preserves me. There is victory—but it must be *His* victory.

We read in 1 Corinthians 15:57, "But thanks be to God, who gives us the victory through our Lord Jesus Christ." Our victory is the gift of God, worked out through our Lord Jesus Christ. Let me repeat it: this victory is the gift of God. It can only be ours when we take it! *Victory isn't something I win, but something I receive as a gift from God.* Just as in the days when we heard the Gospel as sinners, our forgiveness was not by works of righteousness which we had done, but it was the gift of God. Many of us were too proud at first to come and admit our need, and then to receive from the hands of God a full and free pardon for all our sin. But eventually we did; otherwise, we would still be in our sins. So it is with living the Christian life. The deadness that separated me from God still remains, but *Christ is my life.* I can know victory and daily blessing as I relate everything to Him.

We saw in 1 John 5:18 that the presence of Christ is the answer to my sin and temptation. Christ's divine presence within preserves me against the evil. Now we can see that the presence of Christ is the answer to all my service. *Strength for all things—ready for anything—equal to anything.* How wide the horizons become when we relate our service to Christ. We are completely self-sufficient in Christ's sufficiency. I can have all that He is for all that I need. Truly we can say with the psalmist in Psalm 121: "I will lift up my eyes to the hills—From whence comes my help? My help *comes* from the LORD, Who made heaven and earth."

How often have we believed that our help comes from the Lord? We have believed instead that if we did our best, and worked hard, then God would come and add His share to what we had done. In other words, like Abraham and Jacob, *we have believed the promises of God, but made our own plans.*

How often we have reaped a harvest of bitter disappointment and felt the fury of frustration. We have done so much, and it has all come to nothing. Here is God's answer for us—have strength for all things in Christ—and *in Christ alone!* Everything I do bears the mark of death and corruption because "that which is . . . of the flesh is flesh"! But when I relate everything to Him, when I spread it out before Him and commit it to Him, then it becomes *His* responsibility.

Let me finish this chapter with a prayer. Perhaps God has spoken to you, and you want to claim "all that He is for all that you need."

A Prayer of Realization

Heavenly Father,
Forgive my blindness and stupidity. For so long I have tried to fight for You and live for You in my own strength. How disappointing it has been, how fruitless.

How I have limited You. O God, You have promised, but I have planned—and failed.

Now, Father, I confess my failure. I confess that I have planned to get what You have already promised. I confess that I have a nature which is corrupt and dead. It always has been so; it always will be so.

But I now believe that I am a partaker of Your divine nature. I believe that Jesus lives in me through the Holy Spirit. I now believe that He *is* my Life, the only Life I can ever have or need. Nothing less can satisfy; nothing more is possible.

I believe and recognize that He is my victory over sin and temptation. I invite Him to move into every sphere of my life. Grant to me an obedient heart to crown Him Lord of all.

I thank You also that Jesus alone is my strength for all service. I can do all things through Christ Who empowers me. Help me to live in the reality of this. Help me to relate and expose *every* situation to Him Who lives in me by His Holy Spirit.

Heavenly Father, I offer myself now as a vehicle for the life of Christ. I am available. Here I am; send me!

For Christ's sake.
Amen.

6

Limiting God Through Disobedience

We have been considering so far the ways in which God's own people limited Him. In 1 Corinthians 10: 1-4, there are some unusual things said about the children of Israel. Notice the fivefold use of the word *all*: ". . . all our fathers were under the cloud, all passed through the sea, all were baptized into Moses in the cloud and in the sea, all ate the same spiritual food, and all drank the same spiritual drink. For they drank of that spiritual Rock that followed them, and that Rock was Christ."

From the reading of these verses, with the emphasis on the word *all*, we have a picture of a one-hundred percent church—a called-out people with an outwardly united spiritual experience. Any pastor today would be glad if such unity was expressed among his own people, especially if they were eating the same spiritual food and drinking of that Rock which is Christ. Yet when we come to verse 5 in our passage we meet a big *but*: "But with most of them God was not well pleased." In spite of all the outward unity and correctness of spiritual experience, the whole situation was shattered by failure. God was not well-pleased, and they were overthrown in the wilderness. This can be true in our present day churches. We can have that outward appearance of agreement, that unity of purpose, that dependence on Christ for food and drink, and still be displeasing to God. The wilderness is the place where people wander and murmur and are overthrown, in spite of outward unity.

The wilderness is the place where people wander and murmur and are overthrown, in spite of outward unity.

In Psalm 78:8 another cause for limiting God is seen: "And may not be like their fathers, a stubborn and rebellious generation." Verse 10 adds that "they did not keep the covenant of God; they refused to walk in His law." Behind all their outward appearances, there was a continuous undercurrent of disobedience. In Egypt they had been compelled to obey by the whip and cruelty of the taskmasters. But now, having been delivered from their slavery, they indulged in open disobedience in every area of their behavior.

The Challenge Of Joshua

We can follow these people and their descendants one stage further if we turn to Joshua 23. Here we are at the close of Joshua's life. After the death of Moses, Joshua had been called to lead the people into the land of Canaan, and had done his work successfully. Now he is 110 years old (Joshua 24:29). He has had a range of experience which began in Egypt as a slave, and continued on through all the thrill of deliverance by the "Passover lamb." With Caleb, he had joined the other ten spies at Kadesh, and had made the survey of the promised land (Numbers 13:16). He had lived through all the forty years of empty wandering. He had been chosen by God to lead the people in, and to lead them on in conquest of the land that was theirs. All this he had faithfully accomplished, and now his life is drawing to a close.

In chapters 23 and 24, Joshua is moved to bring one last challenge to these people with whom he has lived and suffered and endured for over three generations. He knows their disobedient hearts and how rebellious they have been, resisting every inch of the way. Now he makes his last stand for God, seeking once more to turn these people to the Lord their God.

To do this Joshua, "called for all Israel, for their elders, for their heads, for their judges, and for their officers" (23:2). See how this verse links up with our opening thoughts from 1 Corinthians 10 on the one-hundred percent church—once more *all* the people are being involved. In verse 3, Joshua gives God all the glory: "You have seen all that the LORD your God has done to all these nations because of you, for the LORD your God is He who has fought for you." He goes on to speak of their inheritance and adds, in verse 5, these remarkable words: "And the LORD your God will expel them . . . and you shall possess their land." Here was the promise of future success and of how it would be accomplished. In verse 6 he re-echoes the words God spoke to him in Joshua 1:7: "Therefore be very courageous to keep and to do all that is written in the Book of the Law of Moses."

Finally, in chapter 24, Joshua gets down to business. He realizes it is not good just to talk to the people and to challenge them with encouraging words.

He moves in with all the authority of God: "Thus says the LORD God of Israel." Then God speaks through His aged servant. Notice how He reminds the people of all that He had done: *"I took . . . I led . . . I gave . . . I sent . . . I plagued . . . I brought you out . . . I gave them . . . I destroyed them."* In verse 13, God brings the account right up to date: "I have given you a land for which you did not labor, and cities which you did not build, and you dwell in them."

Then comes the crashing challenge of verse 14: "Now therefore, fear the LORD, serve Him in sincerity and in truth." Joshua is moved by the outpoured goodness and mercy and forgiveness of God. In all the dignity of age and the wealth of experience, he takes his last fighting stand for God: "Choose for yourselves this day whom you will serve . . . But as for me and my house, we will serve the LORD."

As we look at the way in which Joshua deals with a people noted for their constant failure and disobedience, let us remember the instruction of 1 Corinthians 10. These words of Joshua and his handling of the situation are applicable to us today. The same Holy Spirit who inspired the writing of these passages can also speak to our hearts as we read these words. This book was not written to interest people or to educate them, but to be used by the Holy Spirit to change hearts and lives—maybe your heart and life.

A Real Choice

See then how Joshua begins by calling the children of Israel to a *real choice*. They were not to go home and think about it, or discuss the matter, or pass an opinion on the speech. They were to make a definite choice. This is something our human nature tries to avoid. Even in the ordinary things of life, it is so much easier to pass the buck, to let someone else make the choice. It is easier to fall in with a choice made by someone else because, if we get tired of the decision, we can always back out on the grounds that it was not our decision. Joshua knew his people and the hardness of their hearts, so he insisted on a real choice.

It is easier to fall in with a choice made by someone else because, if we get tired of the decision, we can always back out on the grounds that it was not our decision.

He also told them to choose "this day"—not this week, this month, or this year. He wanted and demanded business to be done then and there. This is the kind of treatment we need. We are in possession of all the facts, we know the unfailing goodness of God, we know our own continual weakness and disobedience. It is good for us, for you and for me, to be brought to the point of real decision, of choosing whom we are going to serve. In Matthew 6:24, Jesus challenged the people in His day: "No one can serve two masters; for either he will hate the one and love the other, or else he will be loyal to the one and despise the other. You cannot serve God and mammon."

Our problem is that *we think we can* serve two masters. I am continually meeting Christians in different countries who are busy trying to learn the technique of serving two masters. They do this, and fail miserably, because they have never been brought to the point of making a real choice for God.

It is interesting to study the psychological response of the people of Joshua's challenge to make a real choice. They immediately flung back an answer full of heroism and glowing devotion: "Far be it from us that we should forsake the LORD to serve other gods" (24:16). In verses 17 and 18 they re-echo all the good things that God had done on their behalf, and they end with the pious promise: "We also will serve the LORD, for He *is* our God." One can almost see the horror written on their faces; how could they possibly serve other gods and forsake Jehovah!

But Joshua knew his people. He wasn't taken in by their pious promises and devoted declarations. In verse 19, he unmasked their hypocrisy: "You cannot serve the LORD, for He is a holy God." Their words were just lip service, spoken on the spur of the moment with no conviction behind them.

A Responsible Choice

Then Joshua called the people to face up to a *responsible choice*. Choosing to serve God isn't simply a casual commitment or a pleasant procedure. It is a realization, first, that I am dealing with a holy God. These people were quite prepared to switch their allegiance to God through the saying of a few carefully chosen words. But in Joshua's eyes, they had missed the whole point of his challenge. The holiness of God was that which gripped the mind and attention of Joshua. To him, God was first and foremost holy, and every approach and arrangement had to be made on this basis. Joshua called the people to reconsider their choice, to recognize that the God to Whom they were committing themselves was "a holy God; He is a jealous God."

Choosing to serve God isn't simply a casual commitment or a pleasant procedure. It is a realization, first, that I am dealing with a holy God.

This is also a great truth for our day and generation. The holiness of God is a lost subject in much of our teaching. In many churches God seems to be merely happy, not holy. As long as we all keep happy and things go well, then—who cares! If we today lose sight of the holiness of God, we do so to our own loss, both in purity and in power. We need to be reminded constantly that Calvary was necessary—just because of the holiness of God. In Matthew 27:46 is recorded the agonizing cry of the dying Savior: *"My God, my God, why have You forsaken Me?"* This question was never answered, because the answer had already been given. Jesus was quoting from Psalm 22 in His cry—the crucifixion psalm which gives in amazing detail some of the sufferings of the Savior. It begins with this agonizing question, and the answer to it is in verse 3. "But You *are* holy, enthroned in the praises of Israel." We today, in our response to Christian service, need to face up to this great challenge.

After Joshua had called them to consider their choice and to make it truly responsible, the people replied in verse 21: "No, but we will serve the LORD."

In spite of Joshua's correction, they still meant business with God. His reply is in verse 22. "You *are* witnesses against yourselves that you have chosen the

---

In many churches God seems to be merely happy, not holy. If we today lose sight of the holiness of God, we do so to our own loss, both in purity and power.

LORD for yourselves, to serve him. And they said, '*We are* witnesses!'"

A Repentant Choice

Joshua then challenged them to a *repentant choice.* "'Now therefore,' he said, 'put away the foreign gods which are among you, and incline your heart to the LORD God of Israel'" (vs. 23). In other words, if they really meant what they said in their desire to serve a holy God, then the first thing to do was to clean up their lives. Notice that Joshua called for a two-fold repentance—to *put away* the strange gods, and *to turn to* the Lord.

This is something we often miss in our modern preaching and teaching. We often call on people to believe the Gospel, and what we imply is that they should simply come and accept Jesus as their Savior, the One who died for them on the cross. This is right as far as it goes, but it does not go far enough. Joshua did not *only* call the people to turn their hearts to the Lord. He first asked them to put away the strange gods among them. This is the scriptural order of response to

God. I do not simply come and believe the Gospel. The scriptural order is *repent and believe.* Before I do business with God, I put away the strange gods which are in my heart. This is true for Joshua's time. It is also true in the other books of the Old Testament—and in the New Testament. The Word of God is consistent on this subject.

Repentance was the key word in the preaching of John the Baptist. "Repent, for the kingdom of heaven is at hand" was his theme (Matthew 3:2,8,11). This was also part of Christ's first preaching (Mark 1:15): "The time is fulfilled, and the kingdom of God is at hand. Repent, and believe in the gospel." (Notice the order—repent and believe.) Jesus Christ described His

---

This is the scriptural order of response to God. I do not simply come and believe the Gospel. The scriptural order is repent and believe.

---

purpose in Mark 2:17: "I did not come to call the righteous, but sinners, to repentance." He sent forth the twelve (Mark 6:12), "so they went out and preached that people should repent." Listen to the words of Jesus concerning the joy of heaven, given to us twice by Luke: "Likewise, I say to you, there is joy in the presence of the angels of God over one sinner who repents" (15:7,10).

In other words, actions speak louder than words. *Believing is a matter of words, but repentance is an act of the will and an attitude of the heart.* It isn't the believing that causes the joy in heaven, but the repenting. When

Jesus commissioned His disciples, He said to them: "Thus it is written, and thus it was necessary for the Christ to suffer and to rise from the dead the third day, and that repentance and remission of sins should be preached in His name to all nations" (Luke 24:46,47). The commission is to preach *repentance and remission of sins*—not merely, "Come to Jesus and get your sins forgiven!"

The sermons recorded in Acts show how faithful the early church was in obeying this injunction to preach *repentance and remission*. Peter's great speech on the day of Pentecost ended with these words: "Repent, and let every one of you be baptized in the name of Jesus Christ for the remission of sins" (Acts 2:38). Likewise, his great speech at the gate Beautiful ends with these words: "Repent therefore and be converted . . ."(Acts 3:19). Paul, speaking at the Areopagus in Athens to the philosophers of his day, concluded his message by saying, "God . . . now commands all men everywhere to repent" (Acts 17:30). When he vindicated his divine call before King Agrippa, Paul described it in these words:

"Therefore, King Agrippa, I was not disobedient to the heavenly vision, but declared first to those in Damascus and in Jerusalem . . . that they should repent, turn to God, and do works befitting repentance" (Acts 26:19,20). Notice how the words agree completely with Joshua's "Put away . . . and incline your heart."

The most amazing use of this word *repent* is seen in the book of Revelation. In chapters 2 and 3, the Lord Himself is writing the letters to the churches. When He writes to Ephesus He says, "Remember therefore from where you have fallen; repent" (2:5). When He writes to Pergamos he says, "Repent, or else I will come to you quickly" (2:16). Writing to Sardis He says, "Remember therefore how you have received and heard; hold fast and repent" (3:3).

One final reference in the New Testament is most challenging. We are always ready to use Revelation 3:20 in our gospel preaching—"Behold, I stand at the door and knock. . . ." This is actually part of the letter the risen Christ wrote to Laodicea. In quoting only verse 20, we miss the real point of the words of Christ. Look at verses 19 and 20 together. Christ says, "As many as I love, I rebuke and chasten. Therefore be zealous and repent. Behold, I stand at the door and knock." The invitation "Behold I stand at the door and knock," does not exist without the preceding "repent."

Any response to God, or service for God, which does not come from a repentant and cleansed heart is in danger of being weakened through the presence and power of sin.

These references show to us the great importance the Bible places on the act and attitude of repentance. Notice that this is used not only for sinners, but for Christians too. Any response to God, or service for God, which does not come from a repentant and cleansed heart is in danger of being weakened through the presence and power of sin. There is a tendency today to concentrate on the believing part of the gospel response, and to omit or soft-pedal the repenting part. *Any response to Christ as Savior which does not include a repentance from sin is in danger of producing a weak, colorless Christian witness, which will easily respond to the pull of the world once more.*

Thus Joshua called the people to make a repentant choice. He wanted the quality of behavior which is detailed in 2 Corinthians 5:17: "Therefore, if anyone is in Christ, he is a new creation; old things have passed away; behold, all things have become new."

Joshua wanted the old things and the old ways to be put away, and all things to become new as the people inclined their hearts unto the Lord God of Israel. Joshua 24:24 gives the response of the people to Joshua's call for a repentant choice: "The LORD our God we will serve, and His voice we will obey!" Verse 25 continues, "So Joshua made a covenant with the people that day." How cleverly and positively Joshua had handled these disobedient people, taking them step-by-step and showing them so clearly what was involved in serving God. And how we need, so often, to be shown the same things in the same way, so that our disobedient hearts may be brought to do real business with God.

A Recorded Choice

Joshua had one more step to take before he ended this last great day in his life. "Then Joshua wrote these words in the Book of the Law of God" (vs. 26). In other words, Joshua made it a *recorded choice*. He knew how fickle these people were, how short their memories were. So he recorded their choice, and he also put a great stone under an oak near the sanctuary of God.

"And Joshua said to all the people, 'Behold, this stone shall be a witness to us, for it has heard all the words of the LORD which He spoke to us. It shall therefore be a witness to you, lest you deny your God'" (vs. 27). There was thus the written word and the stone of witness to recall to their minds for all time the great decision made that day.

Many Christians find it a great help to make a record of their decision to turn to God and serve Him. There may be someone reading these words to whom God has spoken in the power of His Holy Spirit. You, too, may have made a real choice this day for God, realizing that it is a responsible choice. Why not make it a recorded choice as well, noting in your own Bible the day you did real business with God.

Choose, Incline, Obey

What we have discussed so far has dealt with the broadening detail of choice as Joshua brought the people face to face with the reality of their condition. It is also helpful to look for a moment not only at the detail of choice they made, but also at the depth on which they were challenged. This is shown for us in three stages. In verse 15 they were called upon *to choose*, in verse 23 to *incline their hearts*, and in verse 24 they promised *to obey*. Notice, in passing, that Joshua did not stop pressing the claims of God until he heard from the lips of the people their promise to obey.

We have seen in a previous chapter that the human heart is sometimes called the soul in the Bible. This is better recognized by us under the term human personality. This heart, soul, or human personality is divided into three areas—the mind, the emotions, and the human will. One or two Scriptures will show this quite clearly. "Why do you think evil in your hearts?" Jesus asked. "Why do you reason . . . in your hearts?" (Matthew 9:4; Mark 2:8). The heart thus contains the area of thinking and reasoning—the mind. In Matthew 15:19, Jesus also spoke of the heart as the seat of evil emotions: "For out of the heart proceed . . . evil thoughts, murders, adulteries. . . ." And in John 14, verses 1 and 27, He encouraged His disciples, "Let not your heart be troubled, neither let it be afraid." The heart thus contains not only the area of thinking, but of the emotions also. But the heart is also the seat of the will. "Daniel purposed in his heart" (Daniel 1:8). So the human heart—my heart, my soul, my personality—consists of my mind, my emotions, and my will. If my whole heart is to be involved in any decision I make, then it must be a decision that involves my mind (my intellect), my emotions, and my will.

Joshua was calling his people to make a real decision for God, and he revealed the depth of choice involving the whole of the human heart by the three words he used: *choose* (vs. 13), *incline your heart* (vs. 23), *obey* (vs. 24).

Choosing challenges the mind. The people had to reason it through and make an intelligent response.

Incline your heart is a test for the emotions. Was there real love in their hearts for God, a real hatred for the evil ways they had been pursuing?

Obey is the final reaction of the will. Having reasoned through the situation and put this alongside the love and devotion they had for Jehovah, the logical outcome was an act of the will—a promise to obey.

This is how a real choice always has to be made. A people who are naturally disobedient, and who constantly limit God by that same disobedience, must somehow be brought to the place where they become vitally involved with God. There must be not only an outward emotional response, but an involvement of the whole human heart.

A people who are naturally disobedient, and who constantly limit God by that same disobedience, must somehow be brought to the place where they become vitally involved with God.

All this is applicable to us as Christians. So often our service for God is based on an emotional response. But we don't sit down and reason it through, counting the cost of doing or not doing the will of God. We somehow never come to the place of taking the plunge and saying "I will, God helping me. I will obey in thought, and word, and deed!" If you have never come to that place, let today be the day, and now be the time, that you decide to take that plunge!

7

Limiting God Through Failure

In the previous chapter we considered the last great day in the life of Joshua, when he challenged the assembled people, and heard from their lips the final response: "The LORD our God we will serve, and His voice we will obey" (Joshua 24:24). It must have seemed so wonderful then, as the people looked back on their failure and forward to their future. "So Joshua let the people depart, each to his own inheritance" (vs. 28), and off they went to enjoy all that God had promised them. What joy and hope must have filled the people's hearts—at long last the tragedy of Egypt and the wasted years of the wilderness were going to be vindicated!

The people went home with the promise of Joshua ringing in their hearts: "And the LORD your God will expel them from before you and drive them out of your sight. So you shall possess their land, as the LORD your God promised you" (Joshua 23:5).

He will expel . . . and you shall possess—this was the divine order for victory and success. God, and God alone, would do the expelling. Then they had to possess that which God had cleansed.

In order to back up the guarantee of blessing, Joshua had told them: "Behold, this day I am going the way of all the earth. And you know in all your hearts and in all your souls that not one thing has failed of all the good things which the LORD your God spoke concerning you. All have come to pass for you; not one word of them has failed" (23:14).

Notice the fourfold use of the word *all*—all your hearts . . . all your souls . . . all the good things . . . all come to pass. How true, and what absolute confidence this should have inspired in all their hearts! This God who never fails was committed to the promise that He would expel . . . and they would possess. So ends the book of Joshua.

The Consequences of Compromise

The next book, Judges, tells us what actually happened. Our passage in 1 Corinthians 10 reminds us constantly that we are to look at these people to see ourselves and to take warning. We can surely see ourselves in these people as they set out with high hopes to make a tremendous success out of life. Every promise they possessed is also ours to enjoy—only in a deeper sense, and with an added spiritual meaning.

Some who read these words will be young in the faith. The thrilling excitement of what God has done for you at the Cross is still fresh in your hearts. Ahead of you lie new experiences and unknown adventures, and you are moving out, as the Israelites did, with a spirit of joyous expectancy. As you identify yourself with their adventure, see now the result of the quality of their faith.

"So the LORD was with Judah. And they drove out the mountaineers, but they could not drive out the inhabitants of the lowland, because they had chariots of iron. . . .

"But the children of Benjamin did not drive out the Jebusites who inhabited Jerusalem; so the Jebusites dwell with the children of Benjamin in Jerusalem to this day. . . .

"However, Manasseh did not drive out the inhabitants of Beth Shean and its villages . . . ; for the Canaanites were determined to dwell in that land. . .

"Nor did Ephraim drive out the Canaanites . . . ; so the Canaanites dwelt in Gezer among them.

"Nor did Zebulun drive out the inhabitants of Kitron. . .; so the Canaanites dwelt among them. . . .

"Nor did Asher . . . Nor did Naphtali . . . And the Amorites forced the children of Dan into the mountains, for they would not allow them to come down to the valley." (Judges 1:19,21,27,29,30,31, 33,34)

How quickly the whole picture had changed—nobody drove anybody out! Notice also that *no tribe possessed their inheritance.* They had to share it with those who were there before. Each tribe repeated, in a measure, the history of the nation when they first came out of Egypt. Under Moses the people came out of Egypt, but they never entered Canaan. They had enough faith to get out of Egypt, but not enough to go on into Canaan. Now each tribe had enough faith to *go to* their inheritance, but not enough to expel the enemy, and *possess* their possessions. What had gone wrong? Had God failed? After all, the promise was that "He will expel . . . and you shall possess." But no one was expelled, and nothing was possessed.

We can find the answer to this great tragedy in Judges 2:1-2, where the account is given of the visit of an angel, or messenger, from God. Speaking for God, he said:

"I led you up from Egypt and brought you to the land . . . ; and I said, 'I will never break My covenant with you. And you shall make no covenant with the inhabitants of this land; you shall tear down their altars.' But you have not obeyed My voice. Why have you done this?"

What a revealing challenge! "I will never break my covenant with you—but you have broken your covenant with me! You said, 'The Lord our God we will serve and His voice we will obey'"(Joshua 24:24), "but you have not obeyed my voice." What a sad and searching question—"Why have you done this?"

God's people did not want to see the end of the old sinful people and their wicked practices. They were more interested in arranging compromises than in carrying out commands.

The answer is plain for all to see. God's people had been instructed to make no covenant, or peaceful agreement, with the inhabitants of Canaan. They had received the command to throw down all the heathen altars. But they had failed in both of these areas. They did not want to see the end of the old sinful people and their wicked practices. They were more interested in arranging compromises than in carrying out commands.

1 Corinthians 10 asks whether this is the way you began your Christian life. 2 Corinthians 5:17 tells us,

"if anyone is in Christ, he is a new creation; old things have passed away; behold, all things have become new." But there are many of us who do not *want* the old things to pass away, and we would prefer that all things not become new—just as it was in this story we are studying. The Canaanites and the Jebusites were far too interesting to be expelled completely. Their altars, their colorful pagan worship were much too exciting to be overthrown and discarded. But this initial step of compromise with the enemy left the seeds of future disaster buried in the soil of human experience, seeds which in later years produced crop after crop of temptation, tragedy, and moral disaster.

Once again, the children of Israel had failed in their promises and in their performance. As a result, God was limited. Joshua had assured them that God would expel their enemies, and they would possess the land. But they were not willing to cooperate with God. As before, the flesh was lusting against the spirit, and all that emerged from the great "Operation Expel" was a miserable compromise which was a disappointment to everyone concerned.

God's reaction to their failure is seen in Judges 2:21-22: "I also will no longer drive out before them any of the nations which Joshua left when he died, so that through them I may test Israel, whether they will keep the ways of the LORD, to walk in them as their fathers kept them, or not."

The Test Of Failure

In this way, God used their failure to test their faith. The situation produced by their disobedience was now permanent. The enemy would always be resident in the land. But when they turned to God for strength and deliverance, to that extent they would be blessed.

This is a great truth we can apply to our own hearts and experience. Many of God's people have failed in their personal living. Their lives, as a result, are shot through with failure and backsliding. The resulting weakness and defeat is obvious and cannot be denied. But there is no need to stay in the place of failure and defeat. God uses our failures to test our faith. If we accept failure as inevitable and incurable, we condemn ourselves to a life of backsliding and barrenness. If, in spite of our failure, we come to God confessing our wretchedness, and seeking His cleansing and His power, then we turn our stumbling blocks into stepping stones. There is still hope of joy and blessing and fruitfulness for all who will see the promise of God and accept the victory which can be theirs.

God uses our failures to test our faith. If we accept failure as inevitable and incurable, we condemn ourselves to a life of backsliding and barrenness.

The first need in the church today is not a widespread revival which will produce more Christians, but an inward revival which will produce better Christians. If those who truly profess and call themselves Christians were walking in all the joy of the Lord, and in the power of His Holy Spirit, they would demonstrate such a radiancy of daily living that God would be unlimited in His capacity to use them. This is our greatest need—to demonstrate *life* through the indwelling Spirit of Christ.

This truth is hammered home again in 1 John 1:8-9: "If we say that we have no sin, we deceive ourselves, and the truth is not in us. If we confess our sins, He is faithful and just to forgive us our sins and to cleanse us from all unrighteousness."

If those who truly profess and call themselves Christians were walking in all the joy of the Lord, and in the power of His Holy Spirit, they would demonstrate such a radiancy of daily living that God would be unlimited in His capacity to use them.

If we will do one thing, then God will do two things. If we confess our sin—not sit and moan about it, or be so introspective that we are constantly taken up with our failure—if we make a decisive move to have the thing dealt with, then God is just as decisive in His reaction. He is both faithful and just—faithful to His promises, and just with regard to His holiness and righteousness. God is *always faithful* and *always just*. The miracle of His grace springs from this eternal reality. Because He *is* both faithful and just, He is able to forgive us our sins and to cleanse us from all unrighteousness. He forgives our sins in relation to Himself in heaven. He cleanses us from the stain and the burden of sin in relation to ourselves. This is a truth unknown to many Christians. They know their sins have been forgiven—that is their greatest joy. But they do not enter into the amazing fact that they are also *cleansed*. In God's sight, they are clean and pure, ready and qualified to go on in His glorious service.

"I will not drive them out before you; but they shall be *thorns* in your sides." This was the Lord's response to His people's failure (Judges 2:3). Isn't this terribly true of some of us today? Our sins and our failures are allowed to remain, and they become as thorns in our sides. The picture is of a man trying to make progress through a barren, desert-like country where the only thing that grows is thorny scrub. As he pushes his way through these bushes, he is constantly pricked and torn by the spikes and thorns piercing his clothing and his flesh. Progress is slow and almost impossible—one bush simply leads on to another.

But this need not be so. God's word is still faithful and just. He told the Israelites, "I will never break My covenant with you" (Judges 2:1). The words of Christ are still as precious and powerful today: "Come to Me, all you who labor and are heavy laden, and I will give you rest. Take My yoke upon you and learn from Me, for I am gentle and lowly in heart, and you will find rest for your souls. For My yoke is easy and My burden is light" (Matthew 11:28-30).

An Example To Be Followed

So far in our studies in this book, we have linked 1 Corinthians 10 with Psalm 78, and have looked for examples and types of behavior which have "limited God." We have seen it in the lives of the children of Israel, then we have seen the same thing in our own experience. In contrast to this, we can turn to 1 Thessalonians for another situation. Paul writes to the Christians in Thessalonica: "And you became followers of us and of the Lord, having received the word in much affliction, with joy of the Holy Spirit, so that you became examples to all in Macedonia and Achaia who believe" (1:6-7).

Here we meet the same word that Paul used of the Old Testament characters—these people at Thessalonica were examples to all that believe. But with what a tremendous difference! In Psalm 78 we saw examples to be *avoided*. Here in 1 Thessalonians, we are meeting a people whose daily living is so joyful that it made them examples to be *followed*. "We give thanks to God always for you all, making mention of you in our prayers, remembering without ceasing your work of faith, labor of love, and patience of hope in our Lord Jesus Christ in the sight of our God and Father" (1: 2-3).

Just as in 1 Corinthians 10:1-4 the use of the word "all" gave us a picture of a one-hundred percent church, so Paul uses the same word with regard to the Christians at Thessalonica—"we give thanks to God *always for you all*." His choice of words indicates the preciseness of his feelings. Paul was much impressed and encouraged by *all of them always*, not by some of them sometimes! These words also indicate the quality of personal and corporate life which enabled the Holy Spirit to say that they were examples to all who believe.

There were three things that Paul remembered about the Thessalonians: their *work of faith*, their *labor of love*, their *patience of hope*. Now look at verse 8 and see what effect their faith produced elsewhere: "For from you the word of the Lord has sounded forth, not only in Macedonia and Achaia, but also in every place. Your faith toward God has gone out."

In every place your faith . . . has gone out. Not merely where Paul was, but everywhere in the Christian world of Paul's day people were talking about the church at Thessalonica, especially about their faith in God.

What three things had impressed the rest of the Christian Church? "How you turned to God from idols to serve the living and true God, and to wait for His Son from heaven, whom He raised from the dead, *even* Jesus . . . " (vs. 9,10). They *turned*—they *served*—they *waited*. These three short verbs give us the example for all to follow. If you compare these three actions that everybody noticed with the three things that Paul remembered, mentioned in verse 3, you will see how the Holy Spirit is especially emphasizing the example we have to follow.

The initial success of the simple Christians at Thessalonica was that they turned to God from idols—which the Israelites did not do. Because of this first step, everything else became possible.

Paul remembered first their *work of faith*. The first thing that the Thessalonians did was to *turn to God from idols*. This was their work of faith—to turn to God from idols. Paul's second memory of them was of their *labor of love*. They had turned from idols *to serve the living and true God*. Paul's third memory was of their *patience of hope in our Lord Jesus Christ*. They were *waiting for God's Son from heaven*. These Christians at

Thessalonica had a faith that worked, a love that labored, and a hope that was patient. What a challenge to us, especially if we contrast their success with the failure we have just witnessed in Judges 1 and 2.

The initial failure of the children of Israel, as detailed in Judges 1, was that they failed to drive out the enemy, and tear down their idols. They much preferred to compromise. Because of this first disobedience, everything else was doomed to failure. They never possessed their inheritance, nor did they truly serve God. Instead, God was limited.

The initial success of the simple Christians at Thessalonica was that they turned to God from idols—which the Israelites did not do. Because of this first step, everything else became possible. This is where these two examples can speak to us at the same time—out of the mouth of two witnesses the truth shall be established. Big doors turn on little hinges, and so it is with our lives. Once we have firmly dealt with the "old inhabitants" in our life, then we have established the hinge upon which the door of Christian witness can turn. Instead of God being limited in our lives, we can go on, as the Thessalonians did "to serve the living and true God; and to wait for His Son from heaven."

8

Limiting God Through Pride

One of the most tragic figures in the Bible is the man known to us as Saul, the son of Kish. He could have been so wonderfully used by God. Instead, he completely limited God by his arrogant pride and willful disobedience.

We meet him first in 1 Samuel 9:1-2. His father's name was Kish. He was "a Benjamite, a mighty man of power." Saul came from a wealthy, powerful family. From his earliest days, he would have enjoyed all the comforts and pleasures of being a rich young man. Verse 2 describes him: "a choice and handsome son . . . There was not a more handsome person than he among the children of Israel. From his shoulders upward he was taller than any of the people."

What a wonderful start he had in life—a rich home, a powerful father, "tall, dark and handsome." He had everything that the world counts necessary for a successful, happy life.

Chapter 10 gives us details about his spiritual life. God was moving in His divine counsels to call this young man out to a position of national importance. Through a series of unusual circumstances, God brought Saul in touch with the prophet Samuel. Samuel, in a speech full of prophecy and prediction, prepared the heart of Saul for the coming events. "Then the Spirit of the LORD will come upon you, and you will . . . be turned into another man . . . for God is with you" (vs. 6-7).

Here, Saul came into contact with God in a new and living way. God was going to be with him in the person of His Holy Spirit. The lovely thing to notice here is the silence of Saul. These were events of major importance in his life. The challenge from God was almost overwhelming, and Saul's response was the silence of an obedient heart. Verse 9 records, "So it was, when he had turned his back to go from Samuel, that God gave him another heart."

Now Saul's physical perfection was enhanced by the blessing of a changed heart. At this time in his life, he must have represented man at his best. There was a quiet humility about him. When his uncle tried to find out what had happened, Saul was silent (1 Sam. 10:14-16). His humility is even more apparent in verses 19-21. Samuel had called all Israel to present themselves for the choosing of a king. Saul was the man eventually selected—but "when they sought him, he could not be found." Imagine a presidential election with no sign of the successful candidate! Saul had hidden himself "among the stuff." Finally they found him, and he stood higher than any of the people. "Do you see him whom the LORD has chosen," Samuel said, "that there *is* no one like him among all the people? So all the people shouted and said, 'Long live the king.'"

Not only was Saul God's choice, but he was the choice of the people also. So Saul, son of Kish, became King Saul of Israel, completing his all-around gifts of physical, moral and spiritual excellence. Here was indeed a king among men, God's choice!

The Failure Of Saul

Now that he was king, Saul was in a supreme position to honor God, to serve Him, and to offer unlimited opportunity for God's will to be done. But from this moment on, there creeps in little by little a spirit of disobedient pride. What could have been a life marvelously used by God became a life where God was limited in every area. God's next step was to test Saul in two special ways—first, by sacrifice. After the joy and thrill of the coronation came the tragedy of calamity. The Philistines gathered themselves to make war on the new king of Israel, and their armies were formidable. Verse 5 of chapter 13 records the chariots and horsemen and "people as the sand which is on the seashore in multitude." God was now going to test the faith of this young king of Israel. Samuel told Saul to wait in Gilgal for at least seven days, and he promised that before the end of the seventh day, he would return. When he came, he would make supplication to God, offer the burnt offering and peace offering, and God would give them victory. So Saul was left on his own with his small army—but with the promise of God.

What followed next was agony for Saul. As each day passed, the forces of the Philistines increased. He could see them from the mountain tops gathering in the valley below—more chariots, more cavalry, more infantry. Not only could Saul see this, but his own army watched with increasing fear and apprehension. Soon the Israelites began to slink away and hide themselves "in caves, in thickets, in rocks, in holes, and in pits" (vs. 6). Some even left the country. The remainder followed Saul trembling.

Saul waited as Samuel had instructed him—one, two, three . . . six days. But still there was no sign of Samuel. Finally, the seventh day dawned, and Saul could stand it no longer. His eyes were now off God, and fixed on the impossible situation around him. In desperation he called for the sacrifices and offerings and, against all the law of God, he who was not a priest usurped that authority, and approached God in his own strength to offer the sacrifice. Just as he finished making the offering, Samuel arrived as he had promised—but it was too late.

How often, when faced with problems, do we rush out and try to solve the whole thing in our own strength, forgetting to wait for God? So often it could be said of us, "You have done foolishly."

"And Samuel said to Saul, 'You have done foolishly'" (vs. 13). Saul had been tested by *sacrifice*, but he had failed miserably. God could have won a great victory that day, but *He was limited by the pride and disobedience of Saul*. God had made him king, but he made himself a priest. In doing so, he sinned and forfeited the right to receive the blessing of God. Saul had the promise of all the blessing, but he couldn't wait for God to bring it in His own way.

Our New Testament passage challenges us once more. Is this the way you and I behave? We have been blessed far more than Saul ever was. He had the Spirit of God upon him, but we have the Spirit dwelling in our hearts and lives. We are told continually to wait on the Lord and to trust in Him. But how often, when faced with problems, do we rush out and try to solve the whole thing in our own strength, forgetting to wait for God? So often it could be said of us, *"You have done foolishly."*

Then God tested King Saul again not only in respect to his sacrifice, but with regard to his faithful, obedient *service*. "Samuel also said to Saul, 'The LORD sent me to anoint you king over His people, over Israel. Now therefore, heed the voice of the words of the LORD'" (1 Samuel 15:1).

Samuel went on to give strict instructions to Saul, telling him to gather an army and lead an expedition against the Amalekites. These people had been a source of constant trouble to Israel, even when they were in the wilderness. If they were allowed to continue, they would be like a malignant cancer in the life of Israel. So Saul was commanded to perform spiritual surgery and destroy the Amalekites completely—people *and* possessions. The command was inclusive: "Now go and attack Amalek, and utterly destroy all that they have, and do not spare them" (15:3).

So Saul departed to perform the will of the Lord. But when he arrived at the place of operation, he *completely disobeyed* the instructions given to him by Samuel. Some of the people he killed, but some he kept alive. Concerning the cattle, "all that was good, [he was] unwilling to utterly destroy them. But everything despised and worthless, that they utterly destroyed" (vs. 9).

Saul interpreted the will of God to please himself, and in so doing he failed once more. God's response was immediate. Speaking to Samuel, He said: "'I greatly regret that I have set up Saul as king, for he has turned back from following Me, and has not performed My commandments.' And it grieved Samuel, and he cried out to the LORD all night" (vs. 11).

When he was challenged by Samuel, Saul demonstrated his departure from God by his lies and excuses. "'I have performed the commandment of the LORD.' And Samuel said, 'What then is this bleating of the sheep in my ears, . . .' And Saul said, 'They have brought them . . . to sacrifice to the LORD your God'" (vs. 13-15).

He blamed the people for the decisions he had made, and he offered God as an excuse. Samuel had to cut Saul down to size, to tell him exactly where he stood. But Saul continued to blame the others, and to suggest that the animals were a sacrifice to God. Samuel replied with these magnificent words: "Has the LORD *as great* delight in burnt offerings and sacrifices, as in obeying the voice of the LORD? Behold, to obey is better than sacrifice, and to heed than the fat of rams" (vs. 22).

The Rejection Of Saul

Samuel then went on the pronounce the sentence of God upon this proud rebellious man: "For rebellion is as the sin of witchcraft, and stubbornness is as iniquity and idolatry. Because you have rejected the word of the LORD, He also has rejected you from being king."

Saul's rebellion and stubbornness had limited God, and as a result, Saul was finished. The chapter continues with Saul still on the defensive, still excusing his rebellion, still refusing to bow his proud will. "I have sinned," he acknowledges to Samuel, "yet honor me now, please, before the elders of my people and before Israel" (vs. 30). Here was a sinner seeking honor for himself and his sin!

What a challenge to us today—*to obey is better than sacrifice.* How often we will make sacrifices to excuse our lack of obedience, giving our money, our time, when all the while what the Lord *really* wants is our genuine obedience to what He has commanded us. Notice that this is how we can limit God. In the eyes of the world, our contributions and enthusiasm may rank high as good examples of Christian living and giving—and all the time what the Lord really wants is to hear us say, "Yes, Lord, Thy will be done!"

How often we will make sacrifices to excuse our lack of obedience, giving our money, our time, when all the while what the Lord really wants is our genuine obedience to what He has commanded us.

From this time on, Saul was God's man no longer. He sat on the throne and wore the crown, but "Samuel went no more to see Saul until the day of his death" (vs. 35). God left him to perish. 1 Samuel 26:21 reports Saul's evaluation of his life in one of his more honest moments toward the end of his life: "Indeed I have played the fool and erred exceedingly." Gone is the boasting pride. He looks back over his life and sees himself as he really is. Saul, who began with so much, is now ending with so little. It could have been so very,

very different, but he limited God for the sake of rebellious pride. As I think of this man, my own heart is challenged and humbled. "Therefore let him who thinks he stands take heed lest he fall" (1 Corinthians 10:12).

God Chooses A New King

1 Samuel 16 goes on to tell the lovely story of how God chose the man he wanted to replace Saul. Samuel, still mourning for Saul, was commanded by God to go to Bethlehem to find Jesse and to anoint one of his sons to be the next king over Israel. Saul was still on the throne, but in one sense he was gone, because Samuel was mourning him since God was quite prepared to ignore him. Samuel's reaction to God's command was one of fear. Saul would kill him. But God sent Samuel under his care and protection. Samuel was sent to anoint the next king, but he did not know which son was to be the chosen man. The account of the choice is an excellent story, full of good teaching for us.

Samuel's arrival caused great consternation in Bethlehem. He was an awesome personality, but he reassured the people and was soon engaged with the family of Farmer Jesse. The Bible gives the names of several of Jesse's sons, making the story much more meaningful. Names in the Bible, both of people and places, have a special significance. The most precious name of all is Jesus, meaning Savior—"you shall call His name JESUS, for He will save His people from their sins" (Matthew 1:21). A person's name was often a guide to his character or work; a place's name often described it accurately. So it was with the sons of Jesse.

The first son interviewed by Samuel was the oldest, a man named Eliab. His name meant "God is my Father," indicating a man whose outward characteristics were those of holiness and religious behavior. When Samuel saw this man, the oldest, with his air of holiness, he immediately thought that this was God's man. After all, Eliab was godly and holy in appearance, so different from what Saul was in his rebellious pride. But Samuel was corrected by God by these wonderful words: "Do not look at his appearance or at his physical stature, because I have refused him. For *the LORD does not see* as man sees; for man looks at the outward appearance, but the LORD looks at the heart" (1 Samuel 16:7).

Eliab looked holy, handsome, godly, and good, but that was only on the outside. Inside, God saw failure and sin.

The next son to be considered was a man named Abinadab (vs. 8). This name means, "My Father is noble," and indicates a person with dignity of walk and nobility of personality. Samuel's reaction to such a man would be obvious. Here was a man who looked like a king! Eliab looked holy, but this man looked kingly. Surely this was the man whom God had provided! But this wasn't God's man either. God looked within his heart and saw nothing noble or kingly. So Abinadab was sent on his way.

The third son to pass before Samuel was "Shammah." This name means "valor" or "courage"— to use a good modern expression, "Tough Guy." Here was a muscle-man, big and powerful. As Samuel gazed on his rippling muscles, he would remember the need of a fighter to lead the people against the Philistines. Here was just the man for the job. But when God looked at his heart, he found nothing that was brave or true, and Shammah joined his brothers.

Verse 10 tells us that Jesse introduced all his sons until he had made seven men to pass before Samuel, but none were chosen. At this point there was a breakdown in candidates, and Samuel asked Jesse if these were all his sons. Possibly Samuel thought he had misinterpreted God's will. Jesse replied that these were all the grown-up sons, but there was still one youngster on the hills looking after the sheep. Samuel asked to see this final member of the family, and so the servants went and called for David. "Now he was ruddy, with bright eyes, and good-looking" (vs. 12).

As David drew near to Samuel in all the fresh, clean vigor of a teenager, God spoke to Samuel, "Arise, anoint him; for this is the one!" The youngest and least important was God's man: David, the shepherd boy. The lovely part of this story is to realize the meaning of the name David—*Beloved*. The other names all drew attention to the outward characteristics of the men concerned, but "David" denotes an inward conviction. Here was one who loved God above all else. This was the boy who later could write: "I will love You, O LORD, my strength. . . . The LORD is my shepherd; I shall not want. . . . I will extol You, O LORD. . . . Bless the LORD, O my soul. . . . I love the LORD" (Psalms 18, 23, 30, 103, 116).

This was the boy who grew up to be God's wonderful king: so human, so humble, so ready at all times to serve the Lord. All that Saul might have been came true in David; all that Saul never was, was manifest in this boy who grew up to honor God in all things.

David Passes God's Test

1 Samuel 16, which we have just considered, shows us God *choosing* a man. Chapter 17 shows us God *using* a man. It begins with a story of abject defeat. Saul is there with all the army of Israel, but they are being defied by one Philistine, Goliath of Gad. We all know the story of David and Goliath, but there are interesting details which illustrate our present subject, "Limiting God," and which contrast for us the characters of Saul and David.

Goliath's cry was not for a battle, but for a man: "I defy the armies of Israel this day; give me a man, that we may fight together" (vs. 10). This was the job for Saul. He was the tallest in Israel. He was the leader. But "when Saul and all Israel heard those words of the Philistine, they were dismayed and greatly afraid" (vs. 11). Eliab and Abinadab and Shammah, David's brothers, were there, but they too were greatly afraid. Verse 16 tells us that Goliath "drew near and presented himself forty days, morning and evening." Saul and his army were being brainwashed by this ugly brute. Eighty times they listened to his taunts, powerless to resist him. Once Saul waited seven days for the Philistines. Now he waited forty days—but God had left him and his army to handle the situation, and his waiting was purposeless.

Then verse 17 tells how Jesse sent David to the place of battle to greet his brothers. He arrived just as the Israelites were moving to the place of battle, and he shouted and cheered them on. But suddenly they all stopped and listened once more to Goliath. As Goliath finished his challenge, the men of Israel fled from before him. David stood and watched an army running away in utter confusion, demoralized and dispirited. He saw King Saul run—and Eliab and Abinadab and Shammah.

David was fresh to the battlefield. His mind was unperturbed by Goliath. His days had been spent with God, taking care of his flock, and so he gazed in puzzled wonder. He began asking questions and making suggestions, expressing his willingness to tackle Goliath. His words reached the ears of Saul, who sent for him. David's words in verse 32 are most challenging—"Let no man's heart fail because of him; your servant will go and fight with this Philistine."

Now the two men face each other. Saul and all Israel are brainwashed, and Saul speaks of David's utter inability to meet a man trained for battle, a man who was nine feet, six inches tall! David recounts what God had done for him in previous struggles with a bear and a lion, and then he proclaims in absolute faith, "The LORD, who delivered me from the paw of the lion and from the paw of the bear, He will deliver me from the hand of this Philistine" (vs. 37). The others were all looking at the same problem—Goliath. Saul and all Israel were saying, "Look at him, look at his size, his power, look how much bigger he is than we are!" David was saying, "Yes, but look how much smaller he is than God!" Saul, the failure, was helpless and hopeless. All he could do now was to continue to limit God. David, God's new man, was confident—all his hopes were centered on God.

Saul next attempted to clothe David in the usual armor for battle. He was concerned with making David strong on the outside. But David took the armor off and pushed it away with these pointed words: "I cannot walk with these, for I have not tested them" (verse 39). But he *had* proved God, and so he was going with God.

The reality of David's faith stands out as he replied to the taunting of Goliath: "You come to me with a sword, with a spear, and with a javelin. But I come to you in the name of the LORD of hosts, the God of the armies of Israel, whom you have defied" (vs. 45). David had his priorities right. Goliath wasn't fighting David; he was fighting God! So David could confidently say, "This day the LORD will deliver you into my hand, and I will strike you" (vs. 46).

David's love was his joy and his strength, and he proved it out there, on his own, alone—with God!

Here was faith supreme. Yet all the time up on the hillside, Saul, Eliab, Abinadab and Shammah trembled with fear. These four men had all been candidates for kingship. One was even then wearing the crown. But all had failed, and *the proof of their failure was their fear*. God was right when He refused holy Eliab and dignified Abinadab and tough Shammah. Their qualities were only on the *outside* after all. But David's love was his joy and his strength, and he proved it out there, on his own, alone—with God.

The rest of the story is well-known—the choosing of the five smooth stones, the use of the simple sling, the crashing fall of Goliath, and the sudden bravery that filled the fearful hearts of the men of Israel. And all because a teenager saw God in the situation!

We often fail to appreciate the matter of the five smooth stones. Why did David choose five when he only used one? Was he unsure of his aim? We can find the answer, remarkably clear, in 2 Samuel 21:18-22. The events recorded in this chapter are, of course, much later than those of our story. Saul is dead and gone, and David is king. There were more battles with the Philistines. Saph was killed in one (vs. 18)—he was "one of the sons of the giant." In another battle in the same place, one of David's men slew "*the brother* of Goliath the Gittite" (vs. 19). In verse 20, we learn that there was still another battle in Gath, and another man of great stature defied Israel. "He also was born to the giant," and was slain by the son of Shammah (David's nephew). Verse 22 concludes, "These four were born to the giant in Gath, and fell by the hand of David and by the hand of his servants."

It is a wonderful thing to learn that a situation only becomes a problem if I don't have sufficient resources to meet it.

Here we learn that Goliath had several brothers. The possibility was that when Goliath fell in combat with David, his brothers might have rushed to tackle David. If they had, David had stones for them. However many giants came that day, David was ready for them. Here was the perfect example of God being unlimited in the devotion of a teenager.

The great thing to realize here is that David had enough resources to meet every possible situation. It is a wonderful thing to learn that a situation only becomes a problem if I don't have sufficient resources to meet it. If I have the resources, then the situation becomes an incident. So for David, the situation wasn't a problem, only a incident. He had all the resources he needed in God.

What a contrast these two make—Saul and David. Yet Saul could have enjoyed all the blessing that David enjoyed, if he had only humbled his will and yielded his heart.

Do you have any Goliaths in your life just now? Situations, or people, or circumstances, that have been defying you for days or weeks or months? Have you been brainwashed into accepting defiance and defeat as the normal life for you? David's God is your God. David could say, "I will fear no evil: for You are with me." Can you say that? Can you go forward into the situation, recognizing the presence of Christ and believing with childlike faith that "greater is He that is in you, than he that is in the world" (1 John 4:4). In this way, your situations will cease to be problems and simply become incidents, under the almighty hand of God.

9

Limiting God Through Laziness

There is a lovely story of a mother putting her three-year-old daughter to bed. She tucked her in, kissed her goodnight, then went downstairs to her sewing. The house was quiet and all was peaceful—for a while. Suddenly there was a resounding thump from the bedroom, silence, then the loud wail of a sleepy, frightened child. The mother rushed upstairs to find her daughter lying on the floor, crying.

In a few moments, peace was restored and the little one was back in bed. Just before she left the room, the mother asked, "Sweetheart, however did you come to fall out of bed?"

"I 'spects I fell asleep too near the place where I got in," was the reply.

And that describes one of the biggest problems in the church today—Christians who fall asleep too near the place where they get in. In a very real sense, this is why so many "fall out" with each other. It is very rewarding to meet a church where the Gospel is faithfully preached and where souls are truly saved and blessed. This is exactly how the church *should* operate. The problem develops when, in such churches, there is a settling down to the satisfaction of being saved, when the general pattern of thinking becomes "Good!

We have heard the Gospel; we have trusted Christ; our sins are forgiven; we are on our way to heaven—we have arrived! This is it! Now we can settle down." The initial occupation with Christ slips away, and instead

> *When people become slack and the vision begins to fade, we become members of an organization, and lazy in living. So we limit God in our personal lives, and in our church life.*

of going on and growing up in the faith, there begins a busy occupation with "things," and with the fringe non-essentials of the Christian faith. People become slack, and the vision begins to fade. We become members of an organization, and lazy in living. So we limit God in our personal lives, and in our church life.

Standing On The Threshold

In 2 Kings 2:1-14, we have a story which has a tremendous message for the present-day church. It concerns two men—Elijah, the old prophet of God, and Elisha, the younger man standing on the threshold of life. Elisha makes a series of simple decisions without realizing that those decisions he makes that day are going to affect the rest of his life. Elisha lives to serve God for fifty-five more years. Nearly two generations of successful service for God came as a result of these decisions. But it could all have been so different, so useless, if he had chosen a wrong way, the easy way. God was unlimited in what He could do in and through the life of Elisha. There were miracles and marvels and mysteries. But it all began when a young man made the right decisions.

God can use His Word to speak to our hearts as we consider this story. Someone who reads these words may be in a similar position. You, too, may be on the threshold of wonderful experiences with God. If you choose aright, the whole future may be a joyous unfolding of the will of God in your life. On the other hand, you may be settling down, satisfied and at ease, lazy and heedless—and God will be limited once more. Our limitation of God doesn't depend upon age, whether we're too old or too young; or on sex or profession, whether we're able and gifted. It depends upon one thing only—whether we are prepared to go on with God.

As the story opens in 2 Kings 2, we find the stage is set for a tremendous occasion. Elisha had been with Elijah for several years as his personal servant, seeing and hearing all that the old man did. Elijah was a rough and tough man of God. He seemed to lack the quality of gracious kindness in all his dealings with people. In this story, there is an abruptness and almost lack of concern in the language he used to Elisha. However, he knew he was soon to depart this life, and he used the events to test the heart and intentions of Elisha. Elijah is always moving on, but always encouraging Elisha to settle down and "stay here." The value of the story is to see and understand the reactions of the young man to these deliberate temptations to "take it easy."

The story is concerned with four separate places: Gilgal, Bethel, Jericho and Jordan. Each was a very significant place in the history of the children of Israel.

Elijah and Elisha are on the move (vs. 1). Elijah knows his destination and the dramatic events which will happen there, but he sets himself to dissuade Elisha from accompanying him.

Stay Here At Gilgal

We meet them first at Gilgal. Elijah says, "Stay here, please, for the LORD has sent me on to Bethel." There was no need for Elisha to continue the journey. He was going to end his friendship with Elijah soon, so here was a good place to settle down.

What I want to do now is to share with you the thoughts that could easily have come to the mind of Elisha, as he was invited to settle down in Gilgal. Elisha was, in a sense, a theological student, preparing for the ministry. As such, he would be very familiar with the history of his people and with the historical significance of Gilgal.

When he thought of Gilgal, he would immediately remember the events we have recorded in Joshua 5. Gilgal was the *place of beginnings*. When the children of Israel at last moved out of the wilderness and into the land of promise, Gilgal was the first place they came to. So, in one sense, Elisha was being tempted to settle down in the very beginning—just like many of us do. We get into the land of promise, we are saved and blessed—and then we settle down because we have arrived!

Gilgal was also the *place of separation*, for it was here that "the LORD said to Joshua, 'Make flint knives for yourself, and circumcise the sons of Israel again the second time'" (5: 2). Circumcision was the sign of separation. As the people were about to move into association with other nations, they were to be set apart for God.

Gilgal was also the *place of satisfaction* (Joshua 5:10-12), for it was here that they kept the Passover, and ate for the first time the food of Canaan along with the manna. In verses 13-15, we have the wonderful story of how Joshua met "a Man [Who] stood opposite him with His sword drawn in His hand." This man had awesome words to say: "as Commander of the army of the LORD I have now come. . . . Take your sandal off your foot, for the place where you stand *is* holy." This was none other than the Lord Jesus Himself meeting Joshua. The *man* could not have been an angel, because He demanded worship. He was divine. God is a Spirit and "no one has seen God at any time" (John 1:18), so it was not God the Father, or God the Holy Spirit, but God the Son.

Think what this meant now to Joshua. Having met this glorious captain of the host of the Lord, Gilgal was not only a place of *separation* and *satisfaction*, but a place of *unlimited strength*. Notice, however, that it was a place of the *promise* of unlimited strength. It was a place of beginnings, where so much blessing and strength were promised. But if we settle down here, all we have are promises—nothing is ever proved. No victories were won at Gilgal, no progress was made. It was a place for feeling happy and hearing promises. No wonder Elisha refused to stay at Gilgal. He wanted to go on, and experience more and more of the goodness of God.

Unfortunately, many Christians today have settled down in Gilgal. We have arrived, we have the blessing, we have the promises. So we settle down and sing wonderful hymns about the promises of God—but we never go on to *prove* the promises. We are happy to quote and re-quote the words of our Lord Jesus: "Lo, I am with you always, even to the end of the age" (Matthew 28:20). But then we go out and live as if not a word of it was true.

Unfortunately, many Christians today have settled down in Gilgal. We have arrived, we have the blessing, we have the promises—but we never go on to prove the promises.

Gilgal would bring other pictures to the mind of the young man Elisha. He would think of another young man named Saul. In our previous chapter we looked at Saul and David. If you check in 1 Samuel, you will see what a significant part Gilgal played in the life of Saul. He was crowned king there by Samuel (1 Samuel 11:14-15). Gilgal was thus the place of beginning for the young man Saul. As we have seen, 1 Samuel 13 records the story of how Saul was tested when Samuel delayed his coming. Gilgal was the place where Saul could not wait for God, where in his fear and anxiety he offered the burnt offering and the peace offering himself. So Gilgal was the place where Saul not only began, but where he also failed.

Chapter 15 tells the story of how Saul was sent to deal with the Amalekites, to perform spiritual surgery for God. He failed once more to do the will of God, and Samuel was commissioned by God to tell him that God was finished with him. Verse 12 tells how Samuel rose early to meet Saul in the morning. He looked for him at Carmel and eventually found him at Gilgal. So that it was at Gilgal that Saul began as God's man, that he failed in sacrifice, and that he was judged by God.

No wonder that when Elijah said to Elisha, "Stay here at Gilgal," he was not in the least interested. What a place, what memories, what a warning to any young man! And what about us? When we settle down where we begin, we fail to go on in the things of God. Where we settle, there we fail, and there we finish— still in Gilgal!

Stay Here At Bethel

Elijah then went on with Elisha to Bethel. We learn from verse 3 that sons of the prophets were living at Bethel. This would be a school or training center for young men. Once again Elijah spoke. "Elisha, stay here, please, for the LORD has sent me on to Jericho." Here was another invitation to give up "going on" and to settle down. There were other young men there. Elisha could join them, and busy himself with their daily activities.

But what memories would the name Bethel bring to the mind of the young man Elisha? He would think surely of the story told in Genesis 28 about another man who was "going on" and who was also at the beginning of his new life. Jacob was on his way to his Uncle Laban's at Padan-aram. He had deceived his father Isaac, incurred the hatred of his brother Esau, and now he was running away from the unhealthy and dangerous situation his behavior had brought about.

Verse 10 records how Jacob began his long weary journey. At night fall he found a place to sleep and "stayed there all night." While he slept, he had a dream which is recorded in verses 12-15. God appeared to him and told him what He was planning for his future. When Jacob awoke, "he called the name of that place Bethel" (vs. 19). Bethel was the place where a young man dreamed a dream of what would happen in years to come. Elisha was invited to stay at Bethel, to join the other dreamers and think about the future. But Jacob didn't stop at Bethel, and neither did Elisha.

The tragedy is that many young Christians are quite happy to stay at Bethel and dream dreams about their future.

The tragedy is that many young Christians are quite happy to stay at Bethel and dream dreams about their future. It is wonderful to think of what might be, and to dream about how lovely it would be if God really took your life and used you, and sent you forth in His name. But if all we do is sit and dream about the future, we limit God. All the great missionary enterprises today, whether at home or abroad, spoken, printed, on radio or television—all these had their beginning in the dream or vision of a waiting, watching Christian. Proverbs 29:18 says that "where there is no vision, the people perish" (KJV). Where there is a vision, there are infinite possibilities for future blessing—so long as we don't stay at Bethel and limit God.

Bethel would also call to mind the story of another young man who was beginning a new life under new conditions. In 1 Kings 11, we have the story of the death of the great King Solomon, the beginning of what could have been a tremendous life for a man named Jeroboam. God had planned to divide the kingdom of Solomon after his death. His son, Rehoboam, was to be left with the one tribe of Judah, and the remaining tribes were to be formed into the separate Kingdom of Israel. God sent a prophet named Ahijah to give this information to Jeroboam: "Thus says the Lord, the God of Israel: 'Behold, I will tear the kingdom out of the hand of Solomon and will give ten tribes to you. . . . So I will take you, and you shall reign over all your heart desires, and you shall be king over Israel'" (vs. 31, 37).

Here was a tremendous promise from God, and all for one man. Chapter 12 of 1 Kings goes on to report how this promise came true, just as God had said. But the real lesson for us is what happened in the life of Jeroboam *after* he was made king.

He had heard and received the absolute, sure promise of God—"I will take you, and you shall reign." But "Jeroboam said in his heart, 'Now the kingdom may return to the house of David'" (1 Kings 12:26). He didn't believe that God could keep it up! He reasoned that when the people of his new kingdom went to worship God at the Temple in Jerusalem, they would change their minds and return to Rehoboam, who would kill him. So Jeroboam thought up a wonderful way in which he could get what God had already promised. There was no need for his plan. It showed an absolute lack of faith in God. But, like so many of us, he tried to help God out of His difficulties!

"Therefore the king asked advice, made two calves of gold, and said to the people, 'It is too much for you to go up to Jerusalem. Here are your gods, O Israel, which brought you up from the land of Egypt!' And he set up one in Bethel. . . ." Then Jeroboam ordained a feast and "made priests from every class of people." He built up a new order of worship all centered in Bethel—an order "which he had devised in his own heart" (vs. 28-33).

From this chapter on, the Bible refers to Jeroboam as "Jeroboam, the son of Nebat, who made Israel to sin." Bethel was the place where one young man dreamed dreams, and where another young man schemed schemes. No wonder that when Elijah invited Elisha to join the other young men also at Bethel, he replied, "As the LORD lives, and as your soul lives, I will not leave you!" (2 Kings 2:4). Elisha was more concerned with a living Lord than with a place of promise!

Stay Here At Jericho

Verses 5 and 6 of 2 Kings 2 tell us what happened when the two travelers came to Jericho. Here was another group of the sons of the prophets. They also came to Elisha to cause him distress of soul. And once again, the old man Elijah told his young companion to stay at Jericho and join the others.

Elisha is now faced with another, more subtle temptation. Jericho was a beautiful place, much to be desired. As he thought back on the history of his people, one memory of Jericho would stand out above all others. Jericho was the place where Joshua led the people to victory. The children of Israel never forgot the story—how they marched around this impregnable city so strong in its walled defenses, how on the seventh day at the given signal they all shouted and the walls of Jericho fell flat, and they marched in and sacked the whole city. This was their great victory. In fact, Jericho was known especially for this one incident. Jericho was *the place of past victory*.

Many Christians today, especially the older ones, stay at Jericho, the place of past victory, and talk about the good old days—and nothing else! Jericho should have a special meaning for Americans—the name means "The City of Palms," and the town was noted for its famous spring. So Jericho carries the image of Palm Springs—the lovely place to which people retire in the winter. When the weather is unpleasant in the other states, it is lovely to settle down in Palm Springs, to enjoy the warm sun, and the absence of bitter winds, frost, and snow.

> *We need to remember that God has no old-age pensioners. Nobody is ever retired in God's service.*

What a picture Jericho brings to our minds—"Stay in Jericho"—the place where you can retire and talk about past victories. And this is exactly what some Christians do in a spiritual sense. They are not as young as they used to be, and following the pattern of the social and industrial world, they start to take life easy and move into a state of spiritual retirement. We need to remember that God has no old-age pensioners. Nobody is ever retired in God's service. All that God does is to "re-tire" us, so that we are capable of further service for Him.

We could do with a new organization in our country along with Youth for Christ—"Seniors for Christ." There are so many jobs which can only be done by those who have years and experience on their side. Thank God for all the older Christians in our churches today. But too many of these dear people have written themselves off as being no good to God. They are each sitting in their own special Jericho. They love to talk about what God did for them and through them in days gone by, but they are limiting God by staying there.

There is work for older people as well as for younger ones. There is need for persistent prayer warriors, for others who can visit shut-ins and bring them the comfort of God. Even bedridden patients can develop a special ministry of prayer and intercession. Letter writing can be a means of challenge for God and comfort to those in need. In all these no great physical strength is necessary, just a quiet willingness to "go on" with God. Remember that Moses was eighty years old when he *began* his life's work for God!

Crossing The Jordan

Elisha was now committed to going all the way with Elijah. Leaving Gilgal and Bethel and Jericho behind them, they journeyed on until they came to Jordan. Notice now what Elijah did to this young man who insisted on going all out for God. He took him out of the promised land, out of Canaan, and into the wilderness. Not only did he lead him to the wilderness—he left him there! True service for God began with Elisha alone in the wilderness. Elijah was taken, but his mantel—the symbol of his power—

remained. If Elisha was ever going to be of any service for God, he had to cross his own Jordan.

Any Christian who means real business for God must come to this experience in his own life. He must see himself in his own true relationship to the plan and will of God. This was no casual day in the life of Elisha—this was *the day*! On this day's decision hung the effectiveness of the next 55 years.

Any Christian who means real business for God must see himself in his own true relationship to the plan and will of God.

So Elisha stood all alone by his own Jordan. Once he had crossed it he would be back in Canaan, not as the friend of Elijah this time, but as the prophet of God. He was still holding the mantel of Elijah, the symbol of his power. But never before had Elisha called upon God. He had had no direct personal contact with God, only through Elijah. Now was his moment to step out in faith, in a faith he had never known or used before. "Where *is* the LORD God of Elijah?" he cried. At the same time, he struck the waters as Elijah had done. God answered his question by revealing His power (verse 14), and Elisha went down into the Jordan.

In a much later day, Jordan was the place of baptism, where many went down into the water to demonstrate a break with the old life, and the beginning of a new experience—a dying to self and a rising to a new life. This was the experience of Elisha. He came into living vital contact with God. He went down into Jordan, symbolizing his break with all the past. He came out of Jordan on the Canaan side—God's man forevermore. He had refused to stay at Bethel or Gilgal or Jericho. He wanted God's best, and he was prepared to pay the price—a recognition of the presence and power of God, and a dying to his own life, hopes, and ambitions.

Continuing To Follow

The Lord Jesus put this picture into words in Matthew 16:24: "If anyone desires to come after Me, let him deny himself, and take up his cross, and follow Me." All the elements of the story in 2 Kings 2 are to be found in these words. *If anyone desires to come after me*—this is the initial challenge of the Christian life. After whom, or after what am I going? Or am I content to be where I am? Elisha was not content to stay anywhere. He *continued following*, leaving behind the ease and the pleasure, seeking only God's best.

Let him deny himself. This puts the finger on the root of all weakness—myself. It is self which demands a constant recognition, whether it be good or bad, holy or hopeless. Self has to be denied, as Elisha denied himself.

And take up the cross—this is the very center of the operation. It is good to pause a moment and consider the words, *the cross.* What was the purpose of a cross? In many churches, the cross is a thing of precious beauty, made of gold and jewels, which calls for worship and adoration. But the cross was not a thing to be worshiped. Some people wear a cross as a symbol of their faith. This is good in a way, but the cross is not an ornament to be worn. Others speak of "taking up the cross," referring to the difficulties and problems they have in their daily lives—their illness, their physical weakness, their job, an unpleasant husband or wife. But this is not what Christ meant—nothing so small as that.

The cross in our Lord's day was used for one purpose only—to die on! It was an ugly, cruel thing, an instrument of punishment which meant death to the one who hung on it. The only effective way to *deny self* is to *take up the cross* and "die" on it. This is the faithful preaching of Romans 6. ". . . we . . . are dead to sin (vs. 2). . . . we are buried with him by baptism into death [as Elisha was in Jordan] (vs. 4). . . . our old man [the self life] is crucified with him, that the body of sin might be destroyed" (vs. 6, KJV).

The natural reaction to this teaching is to say, "Yes, but I'm very much alive. I'm not dead. My 'self' is a real problem!" Verse 11 teaches us how to deal with this problem: "Likewise you also, reckon yourselves to be dead indeed to sin, but alive to God in Christ Jesus our Lord."

Denying self is a day-by-day, and moment-by-moment reckoning that I do not have to sin, to indulge self, to lose my temper.

It is a day-by-day, and moment-by-moment reckoning that *I do not have to sin*, to indulge self, to lose my temper. I count on the fact that Christ has already dealt with my self-life. Jesus Christ not only died for my sins; He died for *me*, in my place. When Christ died, I died. "I have been crucified with Christ

. . . the Son of God, who loved me and gave Himself for me" (Galatians 2:20).

The great word in Romans 6:11 is *reckon*. Its companion is found in verse 13: "Neither yield ye your members as instruments of unrighteousness unto sin: but yield yourselves unto God, as those that are alive from the dead, and your members as instruments of righteousness unto God" (KJV).

There it is—the great word *yield*. I *reckon* myself dead to sin, and I *yield* myself as an instrument—a tool or weapon or implement—unto God. I take my hands off my own life, and allow God to take me and use me as He wills. This is exactly what Elisha did. He "died" in Jordan and came out "alive" for God.

Jesus' last statement here to His disciples was, *"Follow me."* This is the obvious next step in yielding my life to God. It is this *following* which many earnest Christians overlook. They make sincere decisions for Christ and dedicate their lives to Him—and then expect to have gloriously changed lives overnight. They forget that we *grow* in grace. We don't suddenly blossom out into full-grown Christians overnight. It is a slow, steady, growing in grace, a slow steady following Christ. I must moment-by-moment reckon myself dead unto sin, and moment-by-moment yield myself unto Christ. When this is my constant aim in life, there will be no limiting God, no laziness towards God, but a walking by faith and a growing in grace.

10

Limiting God Through Ignorance

I once spoke at a high school in England, confronting the students with the reality of God. In England, the law of the land still states that each school day must begin with an act of worship, and that there must be instruction in Religious Knowledge. This means that there is great opportunity for the truth to be presented. Conversely, there is also an opportunity for the non-believing teacher to present a warped version of the Christian faith.

The school to which I went had three full-time teachers of Religious Knowledge, and all three were sincere, committed Christians. It was because of their love for Christ that I was invited. They warned me to expect real opposition to what I said, not only from the students but from other members of the staff.

It is a strange fact that, in some places, the church has succeeded mainly in arousing a spirit of rebellion and resistance in the young people. I talked about this feeling with the students, and it was obvious in many cases that they had chosen simply to ignore the church and all that it stood for. They complained of the dreary services, and of the fact that most of the congregation were old people who, in some cases, almost resented the presence of teenagers. They commented on the irrelevance of what the ministers preached. They all agreed that there was no "life" about the whole thing—it was a weekly "performance."

Now we realize that this is not true of every church. But it does show one important fact. These young people, and many others like them, have thrown God overboard, not because of antagonism, but because they are utterly ignorant of what the truth really is.

As I listened to their honest comments, I had to agree with them on many things. It was like that when I was a teenager. Services were dull and automatic, and so completely irrelevant to my life as a young man. I remember making the rounds of the various denominations, seeking satisfaction, and in the end giving up the whole thing in disgust.

During my visit to the school, I had many opportunities to speak to the students honestly. I knew that most of these young men and women were ignorant of the Truth. They were passing a judgment on Christianity based, not on God and His glorious provision, but on the performance of an organization.

During assembly, I spoke to the whole school about what the Bible and human experience had to say about them—the students. We saw from 1 Thessalonians 5:23 ("may your whole spirit, soul, and body be preserved blameless") that each human being is a threefold entity of spirit, soul and body. We examined this idea more closely to see how true and logical it is. Our bodies we know quite well, especially in the area of games, sports, and eating! Our souls are provided for through the medium of the school. The soul includes the mind, the emotions, and the will, all of which we educate at school. Then we thought about the human spirit. As I went from group to group later on in my visit, I discovered that this idea was new to many of them. We thought of the human spirit as that unique part of man which makes him *man*. It is the God-shaped blank in every life that never finds true satisfaction until there is a real, personal involvement with God.

It is the spirit that differentiates man from the animal world. No one has ever seen an animal pray. They have no inner urge to worship or placate a supernatural being outside themselves. Animals, for all their interesting ways, do not possess the capacity to know God. Like us, they have a body with which they are world-conscious. Like us they possess, in a lesser degree, a personality—that is, the capacity to use a mind, to show emotions, to exercise a will. But there the likeness ends.

I told the students about my older son who was a missionary with the Sudan Interior Mission in Southern Ethiopia. He had recently moved into a new area to begin a completely new pioneer work. It was estimated there were half a million tribespeople there in one densely populated area. Yet until a few months before, they had never heard the name of Jesus. In spite of this ignorance concerning Jesus, these people were all involved in worship of their own gods.

This characteristic of man is true wherever explorers have penetrated. Wherever human beings are found, they are worshiping some form of a being outside themselves. Man is a worshiping creature. Through the human spirit, man is God-conscious.

We talked of the sense of "seeking" that fills the life of a growing teenager. He is always seeking something, someone, somehow, somewhere—something to fill the growing sense of emptiness. We recognized that the biggest need in the life of a teenager is for something to overcome his sense of insecurity. So much of the trouble caused by teenagers today is the outward expression of this inward seeking. Because young people have so much freedom, the areas of expression are many and varied.

I pressed home the point that only one thing can fill that God-shaped blank—God Himself. We considered the ways in which many teenagers express themselves in this search for *Life*. The desire for new experiences leads many to indulge in sex and drink and drugs—all associated in a way with the adult life for which they are reaching. But such experiences can never fill the emptiness. They only serve to increase the guilt, which in turn increases the need for inward peace and satisfaction. Finally, we considered that the whole purpose of the Bible was to show us how God can fill that blank in the Person of His Son.

This information was new to many of the students. It logically explained their own natures and need, and they listened with increasing interest. Later on, when I went to speak to smaller groups of the students, one question was asked repeatedly: "If this is so, how can I fill this God-shaped blank? How can God become real in my life?" This gave me the opportunity to present Christ as God's answer to man's need. They asked and they listened—and, I'm pleased to say, there was no antagonism or rebellion. They were hearing now, not about a God as represented by dead traditionalism, but a God who had become suddenly relevant to their own experience.

I worked with young people for many years, and I always found it to be true that once teenagers see the relevance of God and Christ to their particular needs, there is no immediate rebellion or resistance. Not every one will accept Christ, but at least they meet Him as the One who still says, "Come to Me, all you who labor and are heavy laden, and I will give you rest" (Matthew 11:28). They are no longer ignorant of who God is, or what He can do for them and through them.

Many Christians have a vision which is weak and dim because of their ignorance of God and His purpose. They never truly apprehend what the Christian faith consists of.

This sense of ignorance affects not only the teenager. Many Christians have a vision which is weak and dim because of their ignorance of God and His purposes. They never truly understand what the Christian faith really consists of. They have only a hazy idea of its nature. They are standing in the right place, and looking in the right direction, but the mists of ignorance and uncertainty produce a vagueness which lessens their capabilities. And so they limit God.

God's Presence, For His Plan, By His Power

Consider with me now, one of the basic concepts taught in the Bible concerning God and Christ. Without a true appreciation of this truth, any Christian life and witness will be poorer. We began this book by looking at the failures of the children of

Israel when they came out of Egypt. Now let us see what God was thinking and planning for them.

After He had brought His people out of Egypt and given them the Ten Commandments, God spoke to Moses about His plans for these redeemed people. Exodus 25:1-9 records the words. The people were to bring offerings of various kinds, but they were to be given willingly. No one should be compelled to give. The offerings were for a specific purpose: "And let them make Me a sanctuary, that I may dwell among them" (vs. 8).

Stop for a moment and realize the greatness of this concept. God's first thought for His redeemed people was that He may dwell among them. The chapters that follow are all devoted to telling of the glories of the Tabernacle, the tent where God would dwell. The idea is repeated again in chapter 29:45-46: "I will dwell among the children of Israel and will be their God. And they shall know that I *am* the LORD their God, who brought them up out of the land of Egypt, that I may dwell among them. I *am* the LORD their God."

Consider again these words: *I brought them forth . . . that I may dwell among them*. Remember that, at this time, these children of Israel were nothing but a gang of freed slaves. There was probably much about them that was unlovely and unpleasant. Many were uncouth and ungracious. Yet it was among this type of people that God was planning to live and make His presence known. He would not wait until the conditions were better, and the people were improved. God's desire was to dwell among His people.

Exodus 35 describes the beginning of the construction of the Tabernacle. There is a continual emphasis on the qualifications necessary for a giver or a worker.

"Whoever is of a willing heart, . . . (vs. 5). All who are gifted artisans among you shall come, . . . (vs. 10). Then everyone came whose heart was stirred, and everyone whose spirit was willing . . . They came, both men and women, as many as had a willing heart . . . (vs. 21,22). All the women who were gifted artisans spun yarn with their hands" (vs. 25). The results of the people's willingness is seen in chapter 36:7: "for the material they had was sufficient for all the work to be done—indeed too much."

The last two chapters of Exodus are concerned with the completion and assembly of the Tabernacle. ". . .as the LORD had commanded Moses" is the constantly recurring phrase. Chapter 40:33 says, "So Moses finished the work." Then God moved in, as He said He would. His glory filled the place, and no one was able to remain within the Tabernacle. Exodus ends with the visible symbols of God's presence constantly in evidence.

"For the cloud of the LORD was above the tabernacle by day, and fire was over it by night, in the sight of all the house of Israel . . ."(40:38). God was with His people. God's *presence* was with them to carry out God's *plan* by God's *power*. God was in the midst, and He was in control.

The rest of the Old Testament is the history of Israel's response to the presence of God. God was there in the Tabernacle. Later He was in the Temple—but always God's presence for God's plan by God's power. Sometimes the people responded to God's presence with love and joyous obedience, especially in the days of David. When this happened, they had peace and blessing and prosperity. Sometimes the people turned away from God to serve Baal and other false gods. Then they experienced tragedy and failure and even captivity, until they repented and cried again to God for His presence, His plan and His power—for God in the midst, and in control.

Jesus In The Midst

This, then, is the truth set forth throughout the Old Testament. Let us see the same truth in the New Testament. John 19 records the awful suffering of Christ, and His death on the cross. "And He, bearing His cross, went out to a place called . . . Golgotha, where they crucified Him, and two others with Him, one on either side, and Jesus in the center (midst)" (vs. 17-18). Here we have the story of *redemption*. Notice the fact recorded about Calvary: *Jesus in the midst*. The same great truth of the Old Testament was being worked out in the New Testament. God in the midst—His presence, His plan, His power. This time, "God was in Christ, reconciling the world to Himself" (2 Corinthians 5:19).

Never think for one moment that the Jews finally captured Jesus and succeeded in doing to Him all that they desired. It is thrilling to realize that, all the time, Jesus was in control. Matthew 26:47-56 tells how the multitude came to the Mount of Olives to capture Jesus. In verse 51, we read how one of the disciples (Peter) drew his sword and started fighting. Jesus stopped him, explaining, "do you think that I cannot now pray to My Father, and He will provide Me with more than twelve legions of angels?" A legion consisted of 6,000 men, so twelve legions would be more than 72,000 angels—all waiting for Jesus to call on their mighty power. But He never did. He was in control all the time. Even on the cross, it was *Jesus in the midst.* As in the Old Testament, our response to this truth is the measure of our faith and love towards God.

John 20 records the triumph of the Resurrection, culminating in the excitement of verses 19 and 20: "Then, the same day at evening, being the first day of the week, . . . Jesus came and stood in the midst, and said to them, 'Peace be with you. . . .' Then were the disciples glad when they saw the Lord."

Even on the cross, it was Jesus in the midst. Our response to this truth is the measure of our faith and love towards God.

Here is the same truth once more. The joy of the *Resurrection* was *Jesus in the midst.* His presence brought the joy. Verse 21 records His plan: "As the Father has sent Me, I also send you. . . . Receive the Holy Spirit." Their response to this glorious reality was again the measure of their faith.

This is seen in the following verses 24-29, where we read of Thomas, called the Twin. He was absent on that wonderful night. For him, there was no Jesus in the midst. His response to the wonderful news was, "Unless I see . . . I will not believe." Eight days later they were in the same room, "and Thomas with them. Jesus came . . . and stood in the midst, and said, 'Peace to you!' " (vs. 26). Once more Jesus was in the midst. This time Thomas met his risen Lord and from his lips came those wondrous words: "My Lord and my God."

In the last book of the New Testament, John, now the aged apostle, is still concerned with the same truth. He was in the Spirit on the Lord's day when he heard behind him a voice like a trumpet. As he listened, the voice began to tell forth great words of revelation.

"Then I turned to see the voice that spoke with me. And having turned I saw seven golden lampstands, and in the midst . . . One like the Son of Man" (Revelation 1:12-13).

Here again is the same phrase—the truth of Revelation is *Jesus in the midst*. Here most definitely is His presence. His plan is seen in 22:16: "I, Jesus, have sent My angel to testify to you these things in the churches." His power is evident in every chapter.

Revelation 5 takes us to the throne room of heaven and gives us another view of Jesus. We read of the strong angel "proclaiming with a loud voice, 'Who is worthy to open the scroll and to loose its seals?'" (vs. 2). John was distressed because "no one in heaven or on the earth or under the earth was able to open the scroll" (vs. 3). Then one of the elders told him to cease crying for someone who was worthy and able.

"And I looked, and behold, in the midst of the throne and of the four living creatures, and in the midst of the elders, stood a Lamb as though it had been slain" (vs. 6). On the throne of heaven was the Lamb of God. Once more Jesus Christ is in the midst. This time He is *reigning*.

The glory of heaven is the Lamb in the midst. No wonder we read in verses 11 and 12: "Then I looked, and I heard the voice of many angels around the throne, the living creatures, and the elders; and the number of them was ten thousand times ten thousand, and thousands of thousands, saying with a loud voice: 'Worthy is the Lamb who was slain to receive power and riches and wisdom, and strength and honor and glory and blessing!'"

What a glorious scene that will be, when the One who was *in the midst on the cross* will be *in the midst on the throne!* And again the great truth is proclaimed. His presence tells forth His plan as he opens the seven seals. His power is the power of heaven in all its fullness.

It will be a wonderful day when we all get to heaven. But before all the wonder of heaven is experienced, there is another glorious day to come. We read about it in 1 Thessalonians 4:16-17: "For the Lord Himself will descend from heaven . . . And the dead in Christ will rise *first.* Then we who are alive and remain shall be caught up together with them. . . ."

Our supreme joy and delight is that we shall "meet the Lord in the air." This time He is *returning*, and the hope of the Second Coming is *Jesus in the midst.* It will surely be His presence that calls us; His plan for us will be fulfilled; His power is the means whereby all these blessed experiences come true. No wonder we are to "comfort one another with these words" (vs. 18).

The references to *Jesus in the midst* which we have been examining have all been connected with events of climactic importance. There is one other reference which is especially lovely, because it involves each one of us. "For where two or three are gathered together in My name, I am there in the midst of them" (Matthew 18:20). This doesn't refer to some great event scheduled for the future, but to the gathering of Christians for prayer. It is the same Jesus, in the same place—*in the midst*. His presence is our only reason for gathering. His plan is that which we seek as we bow in prayer. His power is what we count upon as we close our prayer with the words, "through our Lord Jesus Christ. Amen."

Jesus In Control

So in both the Old and New Testaments, the truth is set forth—God in the midst, God in control. But now we need to be involved, each one personally, as we take this same truth and apply it to our own lives. 2 Corinthians 13:5 switches the spotlight from the Bible to the believer:

"Examine yourselves as to whether you are in the faith. Test yourselves. Do you not know yourselves, that Jesus Christ is in you?—unless indeed you are disqualified."

In this tremendous challenge, see the threefold emphasis on the word *yourselves*. The proof of the reality of my faith is not my words, but the witness of the presence of Christ. A Christian is a person like you and me who has Jesus Christ's presence in him—*Jesus in the midst*. We have seen enough now in this chapter to know that He is there for one specific purpose. He has not come primarily to make us holy or respectable or happy—these may come later. If Jesus is in the midst, then *He is there to control* through His person, His plan, His power—that is, if we are aware of the basic truth of God's Word.

Earlier in this chapter we said that many Christians have a vision which is weak and dim because of their ignorance of God and His purposes. Ignorance of the vital truth that God must be in control produces a weak, feeble witness. This is the ignorance that limits God.

In conclusion, let us look at 1 Corinthians 6:19-20. In this passage we are brought full circle back to the establishing of the sanctuary in Exodus with which we began this chapter. "Or do you not know that your body is the temple of the Holy Spirit who is in you, whom you have from God, and you are not your own?"

Ignorance of the vital truth that God must be in control produces a weak, feeble witness. This is the ignorance that limits God.

In the book of Exodus, we saw the willing-hearted and the wise-hearted providing the means whereby God could dwell in the midst of His redeemed people. Now the truth is complete. We Christians do not provide the material for the temple; we—our bodies in all their weakness—*are* the temple.

The children of Israel, among whom God dwelt, were not rich or important or especially selected. They were just a bunch of slaves redeemed from Egypt. So it is with us. When we accept Christ as our Savior, He comes to dwell in our hearts in the person of His Holy Spirit. He comes to us just as we are. There is no waiting until we are worthy. If He did wait, He would never come at all! His desire is to dwell in our hearts and to make our bodies, individually, the temple of God.

Now we can begin to understand that our own personal history will parallel the history of God's people in the Old Testament. When they recognized God's presence to control—His presence, His plan, His power—then they enjoyed blessing and peace and success. God was not limited. Instead, His will and His Word were sent forth with power. Conversely, when they forsook God and went their own way, they ran into problems, enemies, defeat, and even captivity.

This is the promised pattern for your own life. If you will recognize your body as God's temple, and give to Him that which is rightly His (not only by creation, but by purchase—"for you were bought at a price"), then you, too, will enjoy blessing and peace and success. But, if you choose to retain control of your own life, for good reasons or for bad, in the measure that you retain control, in that same measure you will run into problems, enemies, defeat, and even captivity. This is the basic law of God: "Do not be deceived, God is not mocked; for whatever a man sows, that he will also reap. For he who sows to his flesh will of the flesh reap corruption, but he who sows to the Spirit will of the Spirit reap everlasting life" (Galatians 6:7-8).

Ignorance is no excuse for failure, but it is a sure way to limit God in all His purposes. How wonderful it would be if some of us realized, perhaps for the first time, what is *really* involved in being a Christian. If we choose to retain control of our lives, then we will continue in our weak, sickly, powerless living. There will be no joy in our hearts, no blessing to other people, and we will be limiting God once more. But if we *act* now on the truth we have heard, then blessing will be inevitable.

11

Limiting God Through Immaturity

To those of us who know and love the Lord, the Bible is very precious. We accept it as the inspired Word of God. We remember that many men and women in years past have died for this book, for their faith in it, and for their attempts to promote its outreach. Some of us, however, fail to realize that the Bible is not only inspired in its writing; it is equally inspired in the selection of its books.

Several books mentioned by name in the Bible were equally inspired with the Biblical books, but we have no copy of them today. 1 Chronicles 29:29, referring to the acts of David the King, mentions three books: the book of Samuel the seer, the book of Nathan the prophet, and the book of Gad the seer. Today we have only the book of Samuel in our Bible, but the others were equally inspired. 2 Chronicles 9:29, in summing up the life of Solomon, tells of three books in which "the acts of Solomon, first and last" are recorded. It details the book of Nathan the prophet, the prophecy of Ahijah, and the visions of Iddo the seer. All these were accepted books of God in those days, but we have no copy of them today.

In the New Testament, Colossians 4:16 refers to the epistle to the Laodiceans, a letter from Paul which existed in the early days of the church and was used for guidance and instruction—but we have no copy of it in our Bible today. It is an interesting thought that God was just as careful to see what was kept out of the Bible as He was to give true guidance concerning what was included. Why choose the letter to Colossae, and not the one to Laodicea? When we compare these two places, the question becomes even more pressing.

Colossae, at the time of the early church, was a little unimportant place, a small town in the province of Asia, tucked away in the Lycus Valley. It was a little "nowhere" inhabited by little "nobodies." Laodicea, on the other hand, was an important center for commerce. It was a church that would have been larger, more influential and, in one sense, more important. Then why choose Colossae and omit Laodicea? By our standards today, the affairs of one of our large churches would be much more important than those of some tiny church tucked away on a side street. If we think in terms of our own experience, we can call to mind important churches that draw crowds and have far-reaching ministries. There are smaller places we pass on the road which mean nothing in our Christian experience. This is how it was with Colossae.

The obvious conclusion is that God must have something of real importance to say to us if He included the letter to this tiny church. The Colossian epistle has a tremendous message for every church today, for it deals with the subtle ways in which a church can be true and successful, and yet be limiting God.

Many churches today are active, well-organized, with excellent programs and a successful youth work. Yet somehow, they are not making that quality of impact on the world around as could be expected. Many ministers and church officials are conscious of areas of weakness in the outreach of the church, and are earnestly seeking to meet this need by special programs, by reorganization, by developing new and attractive techniques. But these miss the mark, and the church still continues to limit God. This was the condition of the church at Colossae. The letter that Paul wrote, inspired by the Holy Spirit, was God's answer to the need of that church. So this letter has a message for every church today. Here is a diagnosis of weakness, with the true remedy to restore power and effectiveness.

> *Many ministers and church officials are conscious of areas of weakness in the church, and are earnestly seeking to meet this need by special programs, by reorganization, by developing new and attractive techniques. But these miss the mark.*

If we continue with our study of this letter, we find important information—not only about Colossae, but about the persons involved in the writing. Chapter 4:18 tells us that it was written by Paul, and that he was in prison at the time. We find also that Paul had never been to Colossae and had never met the people. Chapter 1, verses 4 and 7 explain that his knowledge of the place and the people was only by hearsay. Chapter 2, verse 1 emphasizes the point that the Colossians had never seen Paul "in the flesh." The other man involved in this story is Epaphras, a Colossian (4:12). He had preached the message of the Gospel to his fellow townspeople (1:7), and he was the one who, humanly speaking, caused the letter to be written.

At the time of the writing of this letter, Epaphras was with Paul in Rome. He had brought Paul a full report on the state of the church. The information gave Paul great joy. But then, as Epaphras continued his report, Paul was quick to see the weakness in the church and the possible danger which would develop if action was not taken to deal with the situation promptly and effectively. We do not know what it was that Epaphras said, but we do have Paul's written response to the report. Paul's diagnosis, under the inspiration of the Holy Spirit, is the supreme value of this letter to us today. He was careful to analyze the areas of weakness and to give the kind of teaching and advice that would equip the church for a fuller and more effective outreach for God.

We need to bear in mind that most of the Christians at Colossae were Gentiles. This is evident from 1:27 and 2:13, where Paul addresses them specifically as Gentiles and as uncircumcised. (In a sense, most churches today are like the Colossian church—we have not seen Paul, and we are mostly Gentiles.) Paul begins by praising them for the good things he has heard concerning them (1:1-8). Later on he is going to write them strong words that will challenge them and revolutionize their faith, but to begin with he recognizes them as "faithful brethren" (vs. 2), and speaks of their "faith in Christ Jesus and of your love for all the saints" (vs. 4), and of their "love in the Spirit" (vs. 8).

The Danger Of Other Priorities

A study of the letter shows that Paul had analyzed the church's problem into three areas. First, he warned them about having *other priorities* in their faith. These people had been pagans for most of their lives. They had been accustomed to worshiping many gods and spiritual powers—a god for every area of human life and experience. As Christians, they were still caught by a similar attitude. Paul writes: "Let no one cheat you of your reward, taking delight in false humility and worship of angels, intruding into those things which he has not seen, vainly puffed up by his fleshly mind" (Colossians 2:18).

What was true in the church at Colossae is often true in our churches today. We, too, can be involved with other priorities that detract from Christ and inevitably limit God.

Jesus Christ was important to them, but He wasn't all-important. They were worshiping angels and spiritual powers as well as Christ. There were other things and beings in their lives that demanded top-line importance. They had other priorities besides Christ.

What was true in the church at Colossae is often true in our churches today. We can get our priorities wrong. We, too, can be involved with other things that detract from Christ and inevitably limit God in His outreach. For these people at Colossae, Jesus Christ just wasn't big enough in their knowledge and estimation to cope with the needs of their busy lives. Their God was too small, and so they brought in angels to help Him out. As verse 19 says, they were not "holding fast to the Head, from whom all the body, nourished and knit together by joints and ligaments, grows with the increase that is from God." Because they were not "holding fast to the Head" alone, they were suffering from spiritual malnutrition. Spiritual malnutrition is one of the prevailing weaknesses in the church today.

The Danger Of Other Philosophies

Paul goes on to show that because they had other priorities than Christ, they were in danger of having *other philosophies* apart from the truth of God. "I write like this to prevent you from being led astray by someone or other's attractive arguments . . . Be careful that nobody spoils your faith through intellectualism or high-sounding nonsense. Such stuff is at best founded on men's ideas of the nature of the world, and disregards Christ!" (Colossians 2:4,8; Phillips).

If I reject the teaching and authority of the Word of God, then I must produce a substitute from somewhere. So it was with the Christians at Colossae. Having a Christ Who was too small, they also had a Word of God that was too small. They were dabbling in philosophy and "high-sounding nonsense" to support the "new approach" they had in Christian worship.

If Christ is not recognized for all that He truly is, and if other experiences and alternatives are brought in, then there must, of necessity, be the downgrading of the Word of God and the introduction of intellectualism and philosophy to support the new steps being taken. We can be absolutely certain that "such stuff is at best founded on men's ideas of the nature of the world, and disregards Christ."

The Danger Of Other Practices

Continuing his analysis of the situation, Paul went on to warn against *other practices* for holiness. This is the natural outcome of the first two weaknesses. If Christ is not given His rightful place in my life, then I will be taken up with other, less important details. Not having the fullness of Christ, I will need to draw on men's ideas and philosophies for my wisdom. Finally, I will need to draw on other practices for my walk and my Christian holiness. To the church at Colossae, Paul wrote because they were concerning themselves about the outward appearances of holiness:

". . . don't let anyone worry you by criticizing what you eat or drink, or what holy ways you ought to observe, or bothering you over new moons or Sabbaths. All these things have at most only a symbolical value: the solid fact is Christ. . . . So if, through your faith in Christ, you are dead to the principles of this world's life, why, as if you were still part and parcel of this world-wide system, do you take the slightest notice of these purely human prohibitions—'Don't touch this,' 'Don't taste that,' and 'Don't handle the other?' 'This,' 'that,' 'the other' will all pass away after use! I know that these regulations look wise with their self-inspired efforts at worship, their policy of self-humbling, and their studied neglect of the body. But in actual practice they do honor, not to God, but to man's own pride"

(2:16,17,20-23; Phillips). The Christians at Colossae were trying to develop a quality of holiness which, ultimately, would resound to the glory of man.

We must learn at all costs that *true holiness is nothing less than the life of Christ being made manifest through the mortal bodies of the believer* (2 Corinthians 4:10-11). Holiness begins on the inside and works its way out through the yielded life—day by day.

The Christians at Colossae were trying to develop a quality of holiness which, ultimately, would resound to the glory of man.

This, then, was the threefold problem that Paul recognized in the Colossian church. His purpose in writing to them was to deal with this situation spiritually, intelligently, and effectively. Notice that Paul does not attack them, blame them, or condemn them. His whole approach is positive, not negative.

The Person, Power, and Place of Christ

Paul begins his answer to their need by a glorious declaration of the supreme Lordship of Christ. In their eyes, Christ was insufficient to meet their needs, and unable to handle their problems. Paul exalts and magnifies the Lord Jesus. He shows that Jesus is Lord by His Person—Who He is; by His power—what He did; and by His place—where He is. Jesus Christ, Paul states: ". . . is the exact likeness of the unseen God [the visible representation of the invisible]; He is the First-born of all creation." (Colossians 1:15, AMP).

This is Who He is. There is no need for other priorities—Jesus Christ is Lord over all. All that they worshiped at Colossae was subservient to Christ. In these days of turning aside from the truth of God's word, this is something which should characterize and underline all our thinking—*the supreme lordship of Christ.*

Paul continued to magnify Christ by speaking of His power: "For by Him all things were created. . . . all things were created through Him and for Him. And He is before all things, and in Him all things consist" (1:16-17).

This is what Christ did in creation. Notice, incidentally, the phrase "in Him all things consist," or are held together. I was speaking some years ago to a brilliant nuclear physicist who was a dedicated Christian. He told me how his research work strengthened his faith. As he went further and further in his studies of the atom, he was constantly made aware of the fact that there was an unknown, unseen power which literally held the atom together, and consequently held this very world together. He said that for him, this was the significance of the words "in Him all things consist." Not only did Christ create the world, but He holds it together by His own power.

Still speaking of the power of Christ, Paul detailed in verses 20-22 of chapter one the other aspect of His work: "and by Him to reconcile all things to Himself . . . having made peace through the blood of His cross . . . in the body of His flesh through death."

Here we have the amazing contrast in the glorious work of Christ. To create, He only had to speak; but to redeem, He had to die. Because of all the stupendous work that he accomplished, *He is Lord of all*. This is something we need to bear in mind constantly. We can be so impressed by men who nibble at the fringe of power that we lose sight, as the Colossians did, of *the One Who is the Source of all power*.

The third point Paul emphasized was that Christ is Lord by His place—where He is. The Colossians had an exalted Christ but, along with him, they had other supernatural beings. But Jesus Christ is: "the Head of the body, the church, who is the beginning, the firstborn from the dead, that in all things He may have the preeminence" (1:18). "[He] is the authority over all authorities, and the supreme power over all powers" (2:10; Phillips).

There is no one to challenge His position. He is supreme. We need to emphasize this truth in these days. In some of our churches, Jesus is numbered with the great men and great teachers of the world. He stands with Buddha, Confucius, and Mohammed. His words are great words to which we ought to listen. But this is not enough. Jesus is "over all, the eternally blessed God" (Romans 9:5), and His words are to be *obeyed, not merely discussed*.

The Glory Of The Gospel

We have looked at Paul's analysis of the Colossian church's problem, and his answer to meet the need. Another great ministry of this letter is the application Paul makes of his own Gospel. The Gospel they had heard and believed came by the way of Epaphras, who was a faithful minister of Christ. But the ultimate result of Epaphras' preaching was to leave them, as we have seen, incomplete in their appreciation of Christ and His truth. Paul writes to the Colossians about his commission—he was made a minister of the Gospel, "to fulfill the word of God" (1:23,25). It was his privilege to complete, or fully expound, the Gospel which he describes as "the mystery which has been hidden from ages and from generations, but now has been revealed to His saints" (vs. 26). Paul uses the

---

The exceeding wonder and glory of the gospel message is that the Christ Who died for me on the cross now lives in my heart and life in the Person of His Holy Spirit. This is the culminating truth in all the treasure house of God.

---

most extravagant language to focus attention on "the mystery" God wants to make known—"the riches of the glory of this mystery . . . which is Christ in you, the hope of glory" (vs. 27).

The exceeding wonder and glory of the gospel message is that the Christ Who died for me on the cross now lives in my heart and life in the Person of His Holy Spirit. This is the culminating truth in all the treasure house of God. It was this truth that the Colossians did not know, and their ignorance led to their failure. In the church today, this blessed mystery of the indwelling Christ is often an unknown truth, and ignorance of it leads to failure and to our limiting of God.

Now, note carefully how Paul continues in verses 28 and 29. Having established this central truth of

Christ in you, he continues in the same sentence: "Him we preach, warning every man and teaching every man in all wisdom, that we may present every man perfect in Christ Jesus."

Warning, Teaching, Presenting

Notice the threefold aim in Paul's preaching: warning, teaching, presenting. It was a *personal* ministry. Paul uses the phrase "every man" three times in this one sentence. Verse 28 is one of the most important verses in the Bible for preachers and evangelists. Paul—the greatest preacher, teacher, missionary, and evangelist—here gives us the secret of his ministry.

There are preachers today who would rather woo than warn, whose message is all of love, and never of judgment. Paul was a preacher who warned.

Paul began by *warning* every man. In common with every other New Testament preacher, he preached warning and judgment to all. There are preachers today who would rather woo than warn, whose message is *all* of love, and never of judgment. Paul was a preacher who warned.

Paul's second purpose in his preaching was to *teach* every man, a purpose often overlooked in some churches. In recent months, I have had people come to me at different times and in different places, each with the same remark: "I'm not condemning our pastor. He is a real man of God, and he preaches the Gospel faithfully—but that's our trouble. Every Sunday morning he preaches, 'Come to Jesus and get your sins forgiven.' He does the same thing every Sunday night, and if he speaks during the week he has the same message. It is wonderful to hear the simple Gospel, but we want to be taught from the Word of God." Here were fine men of God who missed out on Paul's second aim—not only warning, but teaching the Word. In my years of preaching and traveling I have always found that if a minister preaches and teaches the Word of God with authority, the people will come, regardless of what denomination he may represent!

Paul had one final objective in all his warning and teaching: "that we may present every man perfect in Christ Jesus." Remember that Paul was preaching and teaching "the riches of the glory of this mystery . . . which is Christ in you." So his ultimate aim would be a man or a woman perfect in Christ. The word "perfect" here really means *mature*. Paul was aiming at producing mature believers. He was not interested only in saving sinners, but in teaching them so that they might become mature. This maturity was one based on a conscious sense of the indwelling Spirit of Christ. This is what the Colossian church lacked. It had no mature believers—only saved sinners untaught in the Word of God. That is why it was a problem church with other priorities, other philosophies, and other practices.

This is what so many of our good evangelistic churches lack today—mature believers, with a maturity based on the conscious daily sense of the indwelling Spirit of Christ. In so many evangelical churches there are only saved sinners who are untaught in the Word of God. How we thank God for the fact that the Gospel is preached and that souls are saved! But you cannot build a strong church out of people who are just babes in Christ. You must go on to teach them, and lead them to maturity based on the fact of the indwelling Christ—*Christ in you.*

We ought to challenge ourselves with the question, "Am I a mature Christian? Is my maturity based on the sure sense that Christ indwells me, and that my life is the vehicle for His will?" Some of us will have to be honest and admit that while we may claim to be

> *You cannot build a strong church out of people who are just babes in Christ. You must go on to teach them and lead them to maturity.*

mature, it is a maturity based on wrong priorities. Do I consider myself mature because of the length of my Christian experience, or because of the office I hold in the church, or because I have gray hair, or for some other reason which has somehow satisfied me up to now? Some men I know are rich and hold high office in the church—but they are far from real maturity. It isn't a case of Christ being made manifest through them but of self, self, and more self! Conversely, I have met some wonderful young people who love the Lord with a pure heart, whose lives are crystal-clear in their devotion to Him, and who have yielded their whole beings to His service. These are mature in all the fullness of Christ.

The word "perfect," meaning mature, is an interesting word which is used elsewhere in the New Testament with remarkable significance. In Matthew 19:16-22, there is the story of the rich young ruler who came with his great question to Jesus: "Good Teacher, what good thing shall I do that I may have eternal life?" Here was a young man who possessed everything else in life—wealth, position, youth, social standing—but who wanted the greatest thing of all: eternal life. As the Lord Jesus spoke to him, he was able to show the good quality of his life. Yet he was not satisfied. "What do I still lack?" he asked.

Maturity is based on a personal, intimate relationship with Christ.

"Jesus said to him, 'If you want to be perfect, go, sell what you have and give to the poor, and you will have treasure in heaven; and come, follow Me '" (vs. 21).

Maturity, as described by Christ, is based on a relationship, not with the world and its possessions, but with the person of Christ. This is what Paul was saying in his letter—maturity is based on a personal, intimate relationship with Christ.

The sequel to the story in Matthew is well-known. When he heard the challenge of Christ, the rich young man went away sorrowful. He wanted maturity, but not at that price. You will notice that Christ did not call him back, or lower His terms to accommodate the young man. God has no bargain basement! Whosoever will may come, but we come on God's terms. We can have all the blessings of God to the full, on God's terms. Maturity is only mine when I yield my life to Christ and recognize that He indwells me to use me for His own purposes.

We meet the same word in Ephesians 4:11-13, where Paul writes about the special workers God has given to the church, whose ministry is to teach and lead us "till we all come to the unity of the faith and of the knowledge of the Son of God, to a perfect man, to the measure of the stature of the fullness of Christ."

The Amplified Bible has an excellent translation here: ". . . that [we might arrive] at really mature manhood (the completeness of personality which is nothing less than the standard height of Christ's own perfection), the measure of the stature of the fullness of the Christ and the completeness found in Him." Here again, Christian maturity is shown as a living relationship with the risen Christ in all His fullness.

Colossians 4:12 is an interesting verse, because it contains the prayer of Epaphras, the man who had first spoken to these people at Colossae, who had established the church, and who had come to Paul with the problems of his people. "Epaphras, who is one of you, a bondservant of Christ, greets you, always laboring fervently for you in prayers, that you may stand perfect and complete in all the will of God."

Epaphras always labored fervently in prayer, but for just one thing—that his people might "stand perfect and complete in all the will of God." He realized that only one thing was missing in that church. It wasn't torn with sin and strife like the church at Corinth. There is no sign or reference to evil or wickedness. They just lacked the one great truth that could change their weak witness into a dynamic outreach for

God. They needed to know the living Christ in such a way that they were truly mature.

Isn't this the prayer, the one prayer, needed for many of us and our churches in this day? How about having special specific prayer meetings for the maturity of believers? Perhaps if we prayed more for the believers, we would have greater blessing in the outreach of the Gospel. This is what Epaphras prayed for.

Finally, Epaphras prayed that, being mature, his people might then be "complete." This word "complete" is a lovely picture word used in the Greek text. It means "completely filled," and was often used to describe a sailing ship driving before the wind with every sail up and billowing out as the wind caught and filled every inch of canvas. What a glorious picture of a Christian, a mature Christian, filled with the fullness of Christ, surging on in the Master's business. There is no canvas below decks. Every sail, every means of fullness, is committed to the power of the driving wind. There is no clatter of machinery, no man-made power being used, only the sound of the wind blowing "where it wishes, and you hear the sound of it, but cannot tell where it comes from and where it goes. So is everyone who is born of the Spirit."

So often our churches are like quiet harbors where the ships lie each one tied to his own mooring place. The sails are there, but they are stowed away below decks. There is no driving before the wind on urgent business, taking rich cargoes to needy people—just a gentle rocking to and fro at the mooring. When the tide comes in, there is a gentle rising and a slight disturbance throughout the moored fleet, as they rock more noisily and with more movement. But the tide soon goes out and the boats subside to their normal level once more. As they spend their days moored side by side, all they do is gather barnacles on the hull in a wasted experience.

Wouldn't it be thrilling if some of us would yield our hearts to Christ, and by His grace experience a growing maturity? Then, as He filled our hearts and lives, how exciting it would be to move into a sense of completeness in Him, to raise our sails, cast off the moorings, and move out into the busy seas of life on business for the Master. How satisfying it would be to have every inch of canvas aloft, to sense the filling of the wind and the quiet driving of His Spirit. What a contrast to rocking in the church harbor!

"Also I heard the voice of the Lord, saying: 'Whom shall I send, And who will go for Us?' Then I said, 'Here am I! Send me'" (Isaiah 6:8).

12

Limiting God Through The Home

In the days of the early Christian church as portrayed in the New Testament, the center of all the activity was the Christian home. Paul refers in 1 Corinthians 16:19 to Aquila and Priscilla, "with the church that is in their house." In Colossians 4:15 he greets Nymphas "and the church which is in his house." His letter to Philemon is addressed to Philemon, and to "Apphia, Archippus our fellow soldier, and to the church in your house."

In those days, there were no sanctuaries or excellent church facilities such as we have today, with buildings for Christian education. There were no Bibles or hymn books as we know them. But there was a tremendous power of effective witness and a dynamic outreach—all centered in and radiating from the Christian home.

One of the remarkable developments in the United States in recent years has been the rapid growth of Christian meetings held in private homes. These meetings seem to be springing up independently and almost "naturally," with no apparent human plan or organization behind them. Sometimes it is a special morning meeting for ladies where friends bring friends to meet around the Word of God. Some Christian women have been finding how easy it is to arrange such a meeting, how smoothly God seems to keep things moving, how the most unexpected women will come, and—best of all—how many have come to meet and know the Lord Jesus as their own personal Savior. In other homes, it is a luncheon group or an evening group. Sometimes they listen to a special speaker or a message on a tape, or they study on their own. The ways are varied and the needs are tremendous, but it would seem that God has a definite work to do in the United States, and He is once again using the Christian home as a part of this work. Many problems and difficulties emerge as the work goes on, and not all is as good as it might be, but the home is back once more as a means to an end in the hand of God.

Very often, however, the Christian home can be the one place where we limit God most. A study of the Bible will teach us how important the home is in the eyes of God. *It is the unit with which He builds His church and His people.* A reverse picture of the importance of the home can be seen in the way the Communists view it. Whereas God uses the home to build His people, the Communists seek to destroy the home as a family unit.

I was speaking some years ago with a Chinese Christian who had come from Red China, and who had friends and relatives still there. He was fairly up to date on the state of the nation. I asked him what effect the Communists had had on his country. He replied that for the older people, it was another adverse outside influence. He explained that the basis of all previous Chinese culture was the home—the authority of the home, allegiance to the home, and a natural loyalty to all that the home and tradition stood for. To people raised in this older way of life, Communism was an inferior type of culture. "But," he went on, "when the Communists took over, they set about the systematic destruction of the home as a family unit." The younger generation was taught to despise the old ways and the old culture. They were encouraged to spy on parents and relations, and report acts that were contrary to the new laws of the land. Their allegiance was now to the state and to the leader of the state. On this generation the Communists now had a great hold, and China as it used to be was being torn apart and rebuilt without the home. God builds the home and uses the home, but Communism destroys the home and all that it stands for.

With the gradual breakdown in the home life of the nation, it is all the more important that the Christian home should stand firm for all that is true and pure.

In one area the American people are now destroying *themselves* from within—in the ever-growing divorce rate. In other words, the American people themselves are deliberately breaking up the home as a unit. Statistics show that in the United States, nearly one out of every two marriages ends in divorce. This brings about a definite weakening in the moral and domestic fiber of the nation. America is becoming a nation of people who are fast losing the meaning of the words love, loyalty and allegiance. With this gradual breakdown in the home life of the nation, it is all the more important that the Christian home should stand firm for all that is true and pure.

The importance of the home in the eyes of God is best seen in His arranging for the upbringing of His own Son. With all the world to choose from and every home, rich and poor, at His command, our God chose the humble home in Nazareth as the place where the Lord Jesus should be raised. Not wealthy, not poverty-stricken—just a humble, hardworking, simple family home.

Did you ever wonder how many children Mary had besides her first-born, Jesus? Matthew 13:55-57 tells us that the local people in Nazareth said about Jesus, "Is this not the carpenter's son? Is not His mother called Mary? And His brothers James, Joses, Simon, and Judas? And His sisters, are they not all with us?" We can learn from this that Mary had four more sons, all younger than Jesus. So Jesus had four half-brothers. The word *sisters* implies at least two, but the King James Version is wrong in the position of the word *all* in that phrase. Every other translation or version says "and all his sisters, are they not with us?" "His sisters" could mean two girls, but "all his sisters" means at least three. This gives us at least seven other children in the family besides Jesus, who was the oldest.

This is what God chose for His own Son—a family where there must have been problems and tensions, where the oldest boy would have plenty to do helping Joseph or Mary with the little ones. Consider also that Jesus stayed at home until He was thirty years old—a fact we so often overlook. Tradition says that Joseph died early, leaving Jesus as the man of the house.

There is another significant word in 1 Corinthians 9:5, where Paul says, "Do we have no right to take along a believing wife, as do also the other apostles, the brothers of the Lord, and Cephas?" Scripture records that the four half-brothers of Jesus were married, so He had sisters-in-law as well—and probably brothers-in-law. As the other children married, they would leave home. But Jesus stayed until He was thirty. We can learn two things from this. First, God is so committed to the home and family as a unit, that His own Son took part, to the full, in such an experience. Second, when the Bible says in Hebrews 4:15 that Jesus was "in all points tempted [or tested] as we are, yet without sin," it really means what it says. Jesus knew and experienced all the tensions and pressures of close family living.

Psalm 127 has much to teach us about the organization and development of a home, as prescribed by God Himself. We find here basic principles which are applicable to every age and national culture. The home which operates under these instructions is one in which God's will and purposes will be carried out. But the home which is simply following the pattern set by others in the community is in danger of failure and, above all, of limiting God.

The culture in which we live has developed a wrong emphasis with regard to marriage. The wedding ceremony, when the bridegroom and bride are united as husband and wife, is looked upon as the culmination of all that has gone before. All the glory and glamour are focused on the wedding day. At the end of the ceremony, there is a sense of completion—the whole thing is finally over. Now they are married; everyone can relax!

There is a sense in which this is true. A chapter has ended in the lives of these two. But the whole emphasis of Psalm 127 is that when the wedding is over, then the actual business of marriage really begins. It is this ignorance of what God says about the new relationship that causes failure and weakness in so many Christian homes.

God has a pattern for each Christian home. The world has its own patterns for home-making and home-breaking. The tragedy is that so often we follow the patterns we see around us, and neglect God's pattern. Psalm 127 gives us definite guidance on *building* a home, *keeping* a home, and *using* a home. If we allow the Word of God to speak to us, if we listen, and—most important—if we obey this teaching on the Christian home, then we can know with assurance that God is with us and our home will be to His honor and His glory.

Building A Home

Verse 1 of Psalm 127 gives us this instruction on building a home: "Unless the LORD builds the house, they labor in vain who build it." These few words challenge the basic structure of every Christian home today with their essential truth that there is only one Builder—God. In some homes, the husband is the dynamic character. He does all the deciding and planning and arranging. In other Christian homes, the wife has control. What she says decides the planning and running of the home. Most domestic tensions begin here. But the quiet resentments, the silent struggles for power, the clash of wills and personalities are the seeds of future breakdown.

All this is taken care of in verse 1: "Unless the Lord builds" it is in vain. It is possible to have the most glamorous of weddings, and yet to find married life an ever-increasing source of frustration, for that is what *in vain* can mean—frustration, with all its senseless struggle and waste of time, money, and energy. There is only one Builder, only One who holds the blueprint and decides the detail and structure of the home. He knows the end from the beginning. He promises and guarantees blessing and success if we commit our times and our ways into His hands.

God is always building. He is always on the move, always leading on to new plans and experiences.

There is another half to this great truth in verse 1. There is only one Builder, but there must be two laborers. Here we can fail again in our building of a Christian home. God does the building, we do the laboring—but so many of us don't like being laborers! We would rather do the ordering and telling, and let someone else do the hard work. The laboring can be physical, mental, or spiritual. It may involve a willingness to adjust, to submit, to give way. It often means going without, a willingness to sacrifice time and energy. Above all, it includes a willingness to face reality and a determination not to shirk or avoid responsibility. These words sound good and pious. We all agree to them—on paper. But that isn't enough for God. He wants two laborers who are prepared to take orders *from Him*, and then work to carry them out.

One point we often overlook is that *God is always building*. He is always on the move, always leading on to new plans and experiences. Because this is so, we must always be laboring. The only way to build a Christian home is to keep working at it. This is often where the first cracks appear in a Christian marriage. One member of the marriage either grows tired of laboring, or never settles down to really working, and the whole load falls upon the other partner.

I once sat in on a very honest discussion where husbands and wives were sharing this very problem. It began because one of the men said that in the United States, the women ruled the home—what they said counted most and the husbands had to agree, or else! These words were said with much humor, but there was a subtle sense of resentment behind them.

Then one of the wives challenged the men. What else could they expect? The men shirked their jobs in the home; they left the raising of the children to the mother; they forced the wife to make the decisions. Whose fault was it?

As they continued their discussion, each side added more evidence to the initial points just stated. All that they said was true. These things *did* happen. Some husbands did go off and leave their wives to cope with the domestic situation. Some wives were slack in their home responsibilities. Everything they said proved the truth of Psalm 127:1: "Unless the LORD builds . . . They labor in vain." God, the only Builder, is constantly at work, and we must be willing laborers who are constantly prepared to work also. If we fail in our part, then God is limited in the Christian home.

I have spent much time in counseling with husbands and wives. As a result, I have noticed one area in particular in the marriage relationship which is always in need of laboring. I can illustrate this best in the words spoken to me this past summer by a wife in her early fifties. "My husband is good and kind. He is a very good father to our children. But in recent years, he simply takes me for granted. I feel like a piece of furniture. He never says the lovely things he used to say. I feel so unloved and lonely."

When I spoke to the husband, I asked him if he loved his wife. He looked most surprised and replied, "Of course, I love her. Why do you think I married her?" But he said it in such a way that it sounded dry and colorless and uninteresting.

Laboring isn't always doing physical work. It is often making mental and spiritual adjustments and readjustments.

Since then, I have felt burdened to speak to men about the subject of the Christian home, to urge them to consider their marriage relationship most earnestly. As the years go by, the wife may not be as lovely and attractive as she used to be. The tendency is to allow the affections to become, likewise, less lovely and less attractive. But it is especially then that she needs all the more love and kindness and tender affection. Here is an area where there needs to be some real heart-searching, and where we need to work at it. Laboring isn't always doing physical work. It is often making mental and spiritual adjustments and readjustments.

Wives also need to remember that this is equally as real and necessary in their attitude toward their husbands. As the years go by the husband ceases to be the young, energetic character who first attracted her.

Age slows him down and fills him out. But it is just then that he needs the extra love, admiration, and tender sympathy of the only one who can truly understand him. Every man is still a boy at heart, and every wife should know this, and respond accordingly. In both cases, the blessing only comes when we are prepared to take time to keep on laboring while God is still building.

Before we leave this subject of building a home, we need to be sure that 1 Corinthians 3:9-15 means something real in our experience. Verse 9 says that "we are God's fellow workers." I know this has a specific reference to Paul and his ministry, but the truth is also

The greatest witness for Christ in the world today is a truly Christian home where God is honored, and His Word obeyed.

applicable to the Christian home. Verse 10 says, "But let each one take heed how he builds on it." Notice how personal this is. The words "every one" occur six times in these few verses. Verse 11 speaks of the foundation of the Christian home: "For no other foundation can anyone lay than that which is laid, which is Jesus Christ." The foundation is the *Person* of Christ, not merely the work of Christ. It isn't enough to know that Jesus Christ died for me on the cross. As we have seen in this book already, God's answer to our need is the risen Christ who lives in us through His Holy Spirit. He is the Builder, and by His presence in our hearts and homes, the Christian home becomes a living reality.

Notice also the solemn fact that "each one's work will become clear; for the Day will declare it" (vs. 13). Someday I will have to give an account to God of my work as a laborer in my own home. The following words also challenge us: "the fire will test each one's work, of what sort it is." Notice that the work is not tested for *how much* it is, but for *what sort* it is.

These verses in 1 Corinthians speak primarily of the responsibilities of a Christian in working and witnessing for God in the world as a whole. But we must remember that the greatest witness for Christ in the world today is a truly Christian home where God is honored, and His Word obeyed. The test therefore in verse 13 is "of what sort it is." The success of my home is not the size of it, nor the bank balance behind it, nor the number of cars and "things" in it. God looks for one thing only: what kind it is, whether His building has been matched by our laboring, whether *His* plans are the product shown in our home.

Keeping A Home

Psalm 127 goes on to tell us that "unless the LORD guards the city, the watchman stays awake in vain. It is vain for you to rise up early, to sit up late, to eat the bread of sorrows; for so He gives His beloved sleep" (vs. 1-2). Here the Word of God teaches us how to *keep* the home. Notice immediately the similarity between the building and the keeping of the home. "Unless the LORD builds . . . *unless the LORD guards (keeps)*. . . ." Just as there is one Builder, so there is one Keeper—God.

How true are the words of verse 2: "It is vain for you to rise up early, to sit up late, to eat the bread of sorrows." I have come across several Christian homes where parents rise up early, sit up late, and eat the bread of sorrows—wondering what their children are doing, where they are, and what will happen when they come home—*if* they come home. The ways of God are past finding out, and in some cases the finest godly homes are beset with the problem of wayward children. Many cases, however, which have come to my attention are the result of the failure of the parents to obey the Word of God—either through ignorance or laziness. What can one say to a mother who comes with the pathetic outburst, "My daughter will be a teenager next week. What can I do about it?" Not all remarks are as naive as that, but there is an attitude of mind which avoids taking any deliberate action with growing children, apparently hoping that the children will sort themselves out. This attitude is never the teaching of the Bible which exhorts parents to train up a child in the way he should go, to use discipline, to exert authority, and to expect respect.

A closer look into verse 1—"unless the LORD guards the city, the watchman stays awake in vain"—shows us that there is one keeper, who is the Lord, and one watchman (not the watchwoman or watchparents, but *watchman*). This is God's order and truth, but a truth which is being constantly overlooked and neglected. God's plan for a Christian home is that the husband, not the wife, is the watchman.

The word watchman has the idea of a sentry—someone who is always on guard. The watchman's job is *to watch*, not to fight. In war, when the sentry stands watch, his job is to be constantly alert and responsive.

If he recognizes an enemy approaching, he doesn't go out and fight by himself. His job is to sound the warning so that there can be an effective resistance made by the forces on his side. His job is to watch and warn.

This is exactly the teaching of this verse. The watchman does not fight. It is *God's responsibility* to keep the city. The watchman's job is to bring the power of God to bear on a particular circumstance or situation. In the family, this is the task of the husband and father. He will be on guard as his children grow, watching that which comes into the home—friends, literature, television programs, outside influences— everything which can shape or mar human character. This is *his* responsibility, not the mother's.

God's plan for a Christian home is that the husband, not the wife, is the watchman.

It is at this point where there is a lack in many homes. Either the watching is left to the mother, or the job is quietly avoided. To follow the standards set by non-Christian homes in the community is to ask for future trouble. The easiest way at the time is to do nothing about it—to send the watchman off duty and hope for the best. But this is where verse 2 comes in. "It is vain [absolutely useless] for you to rise up early, to sit up late, to eat the bread of sorrows." Neglect of training and guarding and watching while the children are young will reap a harvest of trouble when they are teenagers.

The watchman's job is to call out the power to protect. When the father recognizes the need and the danger, he should come, with the mother, in earnest prayer to God, seeking wisdom as to what action should be taken, committing the problem to the Lord and taking that necessary action. One sure way of keeping watch is to be constant and regular with the family altar. Let the children take part in the prayers and reading. If they are tiny, the time spent in devotions will be short but to the point, and always practical. Growing children can join in more and more. Part of the devotion time will be, at times, training in recognizing "the enemy." In this way, the watchman will have his people ready to respond to any danger that he may recognize.

Neglect of training and guarding and watching while the children are young will reap a harvest of trouble when they are teenagers.

It should be a warning and an encouragement to every father to read Ezekiel 33:1-7. Here are detailed the duties and responsibilities of the watchman, especially in verse 6: "But if the watchman sees the sword coming and does not blow the trumpet, and the people are not warned, and the sword comes and takes *any* person from among them, he is taken in his iniquity; but his blood I will require at the watchman's hands."

What searching words these are, especially when we put them alongside the words we find in 1 Corinthians 3:13, "each one's work will become clear . . . of what sort it is."

Every father has to answer to God for the way he has watched and guided his children. This is one of the great responsibilities of parenthood. But I can think of some Christian fathers who are doing exactly nothing to watch and guard their children. We need to remember that the example we set before our children is going to be a subject for discussion when we appear before Christ at his judgment seat.

Using A Home

We have thought of *building* a home, and of *keeping* a home. The final section of Psalm 127 concerns *using* a home. The sequence of thought here is interesting—God keeps that which He builds, and uses that which He keeps.

Verse 3 tells us that "children are a heritage from the LORD." This thought needs careful consideration and follows directly from our previous thoughts about the duties and responsibilities of the watchman. Our children are not temporary guests in our home, for whom we care but for whom we have no real lasting consideration. They are an *inheritance* from the Lord. God has an infinite interest in our children. They were His before they became ours. It is our duty and responsibility to invest time and energy in them—not to exploit them as "live" toys provided for our pleasure. As we have seen, as parents we will have to answer some day for the results of our parenting, and the outcome of our training.

Verse 4 has a lovely thought for the truly Christian home: "Like arrows in the hand of a warrior, So are the children of one's youth." Children are like arrows, not like a sword. The idea here is that the arrow can go where the mighty man cannot reach. This is true of many Christian homes.

I remember once being in the home of a fine Christian couple. They showed me the pictures of their five children. All were now grown up. Three were medical doctors, one was a minister, and one was a nurse. Three of the children were overseas on the mission field. What a lovely family—five arrows that had been sent forth out of that home. They had all gone where the parents could not reach! God had built that home, God had kept that home, and now He was using it. But all this did not happen by chance. Over the years there had been much "blood, toil, tears and sweat"—but in the hands of God, and through the outworking of His Holy Spirit.

Verse 5 of Psalm 127 ends with a happy expression: "they shall not be ashamed, but shall speak with their enemies in the gate." The original text does not specify who "they" are. It could be either the parents or the children. The children won't be ashamed of the parents—if God has built and kept and used the home. As a final result "they shall speak with [or subdue and destroy] their enemies in the gate." There will be victory, honor, and glory for Christ. It will come because of two laborers who kept on working, one watchman who continued watching and warning, and two parents who were mindful of their responsibility to invest time, love, and patience in their children.

This is God's picture and pattern for the normal Christian home. Inasmuch as we choose to follow another pattern, then in that much we limit God in our own home. But following God's pattern, in the home as well as in *every* area of our lives, will be productive of untold blessing in the days to come.